THE FISHGUARD INVASION

BY THE

FRENCH IN 1797

SOME PASSAGES TAKEN FROM THE DIARY OF THE LATE
REVEREND DANIEL ROWLANDS, SOMETIME
VICAR OF LLANFIANGELPENYBONT

Dedicated

BY PERMISSION

TO

THE RIGHT HONOURABLE

THE

EARL OF CAWDOR.

CONTENTS.

INTRODUCTION 9

WEDNESDAY.

THE FIRST DAY.

CHAP.
I. THREE FRIGATES . . . 43
II. THE LANDING 54
III. THE FATE OF THE CLOCK . 75
IV. THE PRIEST'S PEEP-HOLE 88

THURSDAY.

THE SECOND DAY

V. DAVY JONES' LOCKER . 109
VI. WELSH WIVES . . . 125
VII. GENERAL TATE'S LETTER . 139

CONTENTS.

FRIDAY.

THE THIRD DAY.

CHAP.		PAGE
VIII.	THE GATHERING AT GOODWICH	159
IX.	THE CAPITULATION	171
X.	TREHOWEL ONCE MORE	180

SEQUEL.

THE GOLDEN PRISON AT PEMBROKE.

XI.	THE GENERAL THANKSGIVING	193
XII.	INSIDE THE GOLDEN PRISON	204
XIII.	AWAY! AWAY!!	222

LIST OF ILLUSTRATIONS.

THE DISEMBARKATION (*From an old print*) *Frontispiece*

STAND OF ARMS IN TENBY MUSEUM. *Facing page* 20

THE FRENCH FRIGATES (*From an old print*) ,, 43

CARREGWASTAD . . . . ,, 54

COTTAGE AT CASTELL . . . ,, 75

A RANSACKED FARMHOUSE . . ,, 109

THE "ROYAL OAK" AT FISHGUARD ., 139

TREHOWEL: GENERAL TATE'S HEAD-
QUARTERS . . . . ., 184

INTRODUCTION.

THE very curious incident related in the following narrative took place nearly a hundred years ago, and, as men's memories are short, and the whole affair reads like fiction—and very improbable and imaginative fiction—it may be as well to write a few lines of introduction, and to give my authorities for the facts mentioned in the story.

In the first place, the evidence of persons who had witnessed the landing, and who recollected it perfectly, and who have told the story to me—I have met many such in the course of my life, as my home was within sight of Fishguard Head. Probably the last of these eye-witnesses was the old woman who died a short time ago—on February 8, 1891. Her demise was announced by the Pembrokeshire papers as "The Death of a Pembrokeshire Centenarian."

The death occurred on Sunday morning at the Dyffryn Cottages, near Fishguard, of Eleanor (Nelly) Phillips at the age of 103. Her age is pretty accurately fixed by a statement she was wont to make, that she was nine years old when the French landed at Fishguard. She was a spinster, and had been bedridden for eight years. When a mere girl she was in service at Kilshawe, near Fishguard, and was driving cows from a field when the French frigates appeared off the coast in 1797.

In the second place, the following books and pamphlets:—

INTRODUCTION.

Fenton's "Pembrokeshire," pp. 10, 11, and 12.

"The Book of South Wales," by C. F. Cliffe, p. 251.

A curious and scarce pamphlet, written by Williams of Crachenllwyd, a place near St. David's; he was the farmer who sent his servant to give the alarm. The pamphlet was called "The Landing of the French," and was, I believe, printed at Haverfordwest.

"The Red Dragon," 1885. *Western Mail* Office, Cardiff.

"An Authentic Account of the Invasion of the French Troops (under the command of General Tate) on Carrig Gwasted Point, near Fishguard, Wednesday, the 22nd day of February, 1797, and their Surrender to the Forces of His Britannic Majesty on Goodwick Sands, on Friday, the 24th of February; likewise some occurrences connected therewith : never before published. Haverfordwest: Joseph Potter, printer, High Street, 1842." This pamphlet was written by H. L. ap Gwilym—and was signed as correct by two eye-witnesses, Fishguard Fencible men, Peter Davies and Owen Griffith.

Laws, " Little England beyond Wales," p. 367.

I am indebted to the kindness of Mr. Leach, the editor of the *Tenby Observer*, for many particulars, and especially for information as to how the news was conveyed to England. He found the following entry in the overseer's accounts for the borough of Tenby:—

"*Thursday, Feb.* 23, 1797. Cash paid by Mr. Mayor's order to John Upcoat, for going out to the Road for a skiff to go over to the English side to give information concerning the landing of about 1,400 French Troops at

INTRODUCTION.

Fishguard in the County, who on the next day surrendered themselves up to the Welsh &c., that went to oppose them as *prisoners of war*, and were marched accordingly by Saturday 25th to Haverfordwest ... 1s."

This entry could not have been entirely made on Feb. 23rd, unless the worthy overseer had the gift of prophecy.

The messenger probably came on to Tenby from Stackpole, where he aroused Lord Cawdor with the tidings in the middle of Wednesday night. The news conveyed by John Upcoat must have been taken across the Channel to Somersetshire and thence to London; the manner of proceeding at the *fin de siècle* of the eighteenth century contrasts amusingly with the rapidity of the nineteenth, but possibly our time will be scoffed at and considered slow by the twentieth.

The *European Magazine* of the period

gives the names of the vessels: *La Résistance*, commanded by Monsieur Montague, 40 guns, eighteen pounders on her main deck, 345 men. The other frigate *La Constance*, commanded by Monsieur Desauny, mounted 24 nine-pounders on her main deck, with 189 men.[1]

One of the frigates and the corvette were eventually captured off Brest by the *St. Fiorenzo* frigate (Captain Sir H. B. Neale, Bart.) and the *La Nymphe* (Captain J. Cooke), who took them both into Portsmouth, where the frigate was repaired and rechristened the *Fisgard*, presumably the French pronunciation of Fishguard, and was until quite lately the receiving ship at Sheerness. The other frigate and the lugger managed to get safely into Brest.

The officers present at the council of war held at the "Royal Oak," Fishguard, were

[1] Laws, "Little England beyond Wales."

INTRODUCTION. 15

the Lord-Lieutenant of the county, Lord Milford (who from age and infirmity had given up the command of the troops to Lord Cawdor), Lord Cawdor, Colonel Knox, Colonel Colby, Major Ackland, Colonel Dan. Vaughan, Colonel James, Colonel George Vaughan, the governor of Fishguard Fort, and other gentlemen. The troops consisted of the Castle Martin Yeomanry Cavalry, the Cardiganshire Militia, the Cardiff Militia (which was then stationed in Pembrokeshire), some Fencible infantry, and a few sailors under Lieutenants Mears and Perkins, in all 750 men.

The letters that passed between General Tate and Lord Cawdor are given in the narrative, but the following letters from Lord Milford and Lord Cawdor to the Duke of Portland, Secretary of State for the Home Department, may be found interesting :—

From Lord Milford.

"HAVERFORDWEST,

"*February* 26, 1797, Six o'clock A.M.

"Since I had the honour of writing last to your Grace by express I received information of the French ships having sailed and left 300 men behind, who have surrendered themselves prisoners. The great spirit and loyalty that the gentlemen and peasantry has shown on this occasion exceeds description. Many thousands of the latter assembled, armed with pikes and scythes, and attacked the enemy previous to the arrival of troops that were sent against them."

"HAVERFORDWEST,

"*February* 24, Nine o'clock P.M.

"I have the honour and pleasure to inform your Grace that the whole of the French troops, amounting to near fourteen hundred men, have surrendered, and are now on their march to Haverfordwest. I have taken the first opportunity of announcing the good news to your Grace, and shall have the honour of writing again to your Grace by tomorrow's post."

The following letter was written by Lord Cawdor to the Duke of Portland :—

"FISHGUARD,

"*Friday, February* 24, 1797.

"MY LORD,—In consequence of having received information on Wednesday night, at eleven o'clock, that three large ships of war and a lugger had anchored in a small roadstead upon the coast, in the neighbourhood of this town, I proceeded immediately with a detachment of the Cardiganshire Militia and all the provincial force I could collect to the place. I soon gained positive intelligence they had disembarked about 1,200 men, but no cannon. Upon the night setting in a French officer, whom I found to be second in command, came in with a letter (a copy of which I sent your Grace, together with my answer [1]), in consequence of which they determined to surrender themselves prisoners of war, and, accordingly, laid down their arms this day at two o'clock. I cannot, at this moment, inform your Grace the exact number of prisoners, but I believe it to be their whole force. It is my intention to march them this night to Haverfordwest, where I shall make the best distribution in my power. The frigates, corvette, and lugger got under weigh yesterday evening, and were this morning entirely out of sight. The fatigue we experienced will, I trust, excuse me to your Grace for not giving a more particular detail ; but my anxiety to do justice to the officers and men I had the honour to command, will induce me to

[1] These letters are given in the narrative.

INTRODUCTION.

attend your Grace with as little delay as possible, to state their merits and, at the same time, to give you every information in my power on this subject. The spirit and loyalty which has pervaded all ranks throughout the country is infinitely beyond what I can express.

"I am, &c.,
"CAWDOR."

Lord Cawdor's "distribution" took the form of placing 700 men in the beautiful old church of St. Mary's (which they greatly injured), 500 in the Town Hall, and the remainder in the store-houses of Haverfordwest. The officers were allowed out on parole, and one of them showed scant respect for his word of honour, for he was discovered at a silversmith's trying to barter an old silver cup for coin of the realm, with which doubtless to escape to France. There were some letters on the cup which he chose to decipher as "La Vendée"; they turned out on inspection to be "Llanwnda," from which church the chalice had been stolen, and where it was at once returned, while the officer was transferred from the "Castle Hotel" to the Castle jail—a very different place.

A number of the prisoners were shortly after sent on to Carmarthen and to Pembroke, where the romantic episode of the escape from the Golden Prison occurred exactly as given in the narrative. The arms and ammunition taken from the French filled fifty-five carts; their muskets were the ordinary weapon of the period, with flint locks, barrels 3ft. 7in., whole length 4ft. 10in., weight 9¾lbs. Lord Cawdor presented two of these muskets to the Tenby Museum, and Mr. Mathias gave a short sword and scabbard. On each side of the sword are repre-

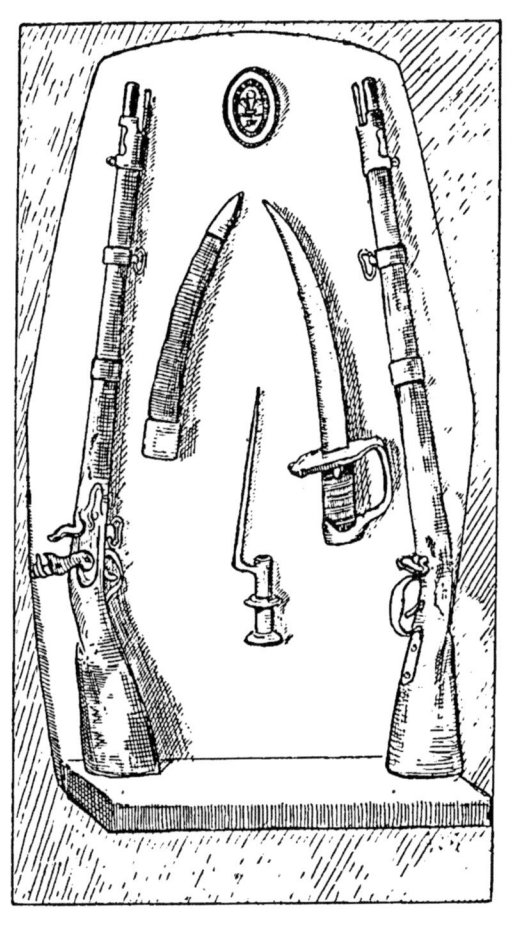

STAND OF ARMS IN TENBY MUSEUM.

sented sun, moon, and stars, with the inscription *Cassagnard, Fourbisseur du Roy, Nantes.* There are half-a-dozen cannonballs — nine pounders — at the house of Eleanor Rees, of Goodwick, which were given to her father by the French—a curious toy for a small boy of two or three years of age. The invaders seem to have been very kind to this young Taffy, nursed him on their knees, and made much of him, and finally presented him with this strange *gage d'amour.* He was probably a plucky little fellow, for he grew into a brave man, and was awarded a medal for having at various times saved many lives, going out in his own boat to shipwrecked vessels and rescuing the crews—when the *Lady Kenmare* foundered he saved, among others, two ladies and some children, bringing them through a tremendous sea, "in their night-dresses, as wet as sops," the narrator added.

Most of the prisoners were finally sent back to France, when it was discovered what manner of men they were. Lord Cawdor took General Tate and some of the other officers to London, whence they were consigned to Dartmoor. This personally-conducted journey through England was not without peril. The people were greatly incensed against the French, and were quite ready to carry out Lynch law on these unhappy men, and in the excitement of the moment a mob does not always discriminate between its friends and its foes. It was fortunate for Tate and his fellows, and still more fortunate for Pembrokeshire, that the conduct of the whole affair from first to last was in such able and determined hands as those of Lord Cawdor. A letter from him to Lady Cawdor (hitherto unpublished, and for which I am indebted to Mr. Laws), gives a very vivid account of this journey.

INTRODUCTION.

"OXFORD STREET,

"*Monday morn, March* 13, 1797.

"I have at length the satisfaction of an hour's time free from interruption to give you a short account of our employment, &c., since I quitted you, but shall reserve much of the detail for your amusement when we meet, a moment I ardently long for. Near Tavern Spite I met a messenger, with the D. of Portland's despatches to me signifying the King's approbation of my conduct, which probably General Rooke has shown you, accompanied also by a handsome and flattering private letter from the Duke. Upon my arrival at Carmarthen I immediately sent off the messenger with my letters, and finding the impossibility of procuring horses until the following morn was in the expectation of getting a quiet night, having procured a bed at a private house; but an alarm of a fire in the town joined to confusion created by the report of a landing in great force in Glamorganshire, which I knew must have no foundation, prevented my obtaining sleep for one moment. Early in the morn we left Carmarthen, with three chaises; in the first, Joe Adams had charge of Tate and Captain Tyrell, the first alarmed and confused, the second a stupid Paddy. I had Le Brun with me, as dirty as a pig, but more intelligent and better manners; in the last, Lord E. Somerset had the care of Captain Norris and Lieutenant St. Leger, both greatly frightened, they had but little conversation. The whole road we passed through great crowds of people at all the places were (*sic*) we changed horses, and thro' Wales tho' the indignation of the people was great, I found my influence would protect them without difficulty. The women were more clamorous than the men, making signs to cut their throats, and desiring I would not take the trouble of carrying them further. All the military assistance I could get at Oxford as a guard for the night was a sergeant of your friend and landlord, and two recruits, but I had no apprehension of their escape as their remain (*sic*) with us was the only thing that ensured their safety. At Uxbridge the rage of the mob was chiefly directed against Tate, who was supposed to be Wall, and he trembled almost to convulsions, by a little arrangement I contrived to bring them quiet through the parks, and lodged them in the Duke of Portland's before any crowd was assembled. My time since that moment has been taken up with attendance at the different offices, &c., and ministers are so bewildered by the difficulties at the Bank, &c., that it is more than usually difficult to get access to them for any time, but I have seen them all and stated to them plainly and decidedly, the situation of Pembroke, &c.,

giving every testimony in my power. The weather is extremely cold, the town I hear dull and unpleasant, everybody I have seen much interested about you, Mrs. Wodehouse . . . and desires her love. Joe his respects."

[No signature.]

Having disposed of the rank and file of the expedition, there comes the natural question, what was its *raison d'être ?* Some persons think it was merely a fine stroke of political economy on the part of the French Government, for a considerable number of the men were convicts, and to have them killed or imprisoned at the expense of the English would undoubtedly have been a good financial arrangement; but the biography of Lazare Hoche[1] proves that a much larger idea than this was in the mind

[1] "Biographie de Lazare Hoche," par Emile de Bonnechose. Hachette, Paris.

INTRODUCTION.

of the originator of the invasion. He was a successful general and an ambitious man, and his imagination was fired by the prowess of Napoleon :—" La France couvrait alors ses frontières de jeunes républiques, et Bonaparte saisissait les imaginations par ses merveilleux exploits en Italie. Hoche, retenu par les pénibles soins de la pacification de l'Ouest, avait suivi de son ardente pensée le vainqueur d'Arcole à travers, tous ses champs de victoire : 'Glorieux jeune homme, s'écriait-il en se frappant le front,' que je te porte envie! Il brûlait de faire d'aussi grandes choses, et de trouver un champ de gloire digne de son génie; il projetait donc de révolutionner l'Irlande, de la transformer en république ; puis de passer en Angleterre et de la frapper au cœur. Il fit adopter son projet par le gouvernement qui, après s'être concerté avec les chefs des révolutionnaires irlandais, prépara à Brest une grande expédition dont

Hoche eut le commandement.... Hoche y joignit deux légions, qu'il nomma légions des Francs : il composa la première des officiers et des soldats les plus résolus, audacieux jusqu' à la témérité ; il forma la seconde, il faut le dire, d'éléments indignes, et c'est un reproche pour sa mémoire. Détestant l'Angleterre, partageant de tristes prejujés et regardant, en haine du gouvernement britannique, le peuple anglais comme le suppôt de ministres perfides et d'une odieuse aristocratie, tous les moyens lui semblaient permis pour abaisser et pour désoler cette fière nation : il agit en conséquence et fit entrer dans cette seconde légion tout ce qu'il put ramasser de gens perdus, de bandits et de massacreurs, et il la mit sous le commandement d'un chef étranger connu par sa sauvage énergie. Cette légion devait aborder en Angleterre pour abuser l'ennemi sur la véritable destination de l'escadre portant le corps expeditionnaire: elle eut l'ordre de débarquer à l'embouchure de la Saverne, de se porter de nuit sur Bristol, d'incendier cette ville et de semer la devastation dans les campagnes environnantes ; puis de se rembarquer pour jeter plusieurs détachements sur différents points du littoral en portant partout la mort, le ravage et l'incendie, attirant ainsi sur elle et retenant en Angleterre une partie considérable des forces britanniques, tandis que l'expédition cinglerait vers la côte irlandaise."

In the appendix of the same work we find the source from which Hoche compiled his instructions.

"Note D.

"Extrait du projet de Carnot pour l'organisation d'une chouaunnerie en Angleterre, et dans lequel Hoche puisa les instructions données par lui à la seconde légion des Francs.

"Les hommes employés à cette expédition devront être, autant que faire se pourra, jeunes, robustes, audacieux, d'une âme accessible à l'appât du butin.

"Il faut qu'à l'exemple de ce que faisaient les filibustiers dans les Antilles, ils sachent porter, au milieu de leurs ennemis, l'épouvante et la mort.

. . . . .

"On pourrait incorporer dans ces troupes les condamnés par jugement aux fers ou à la chaine en qui l'on reconnaîtrait les dispositions physiques et morales requises pour les individus employés à cette expédition. On assurerait à ces individus la possession du butin qu'ils feraient. On leur en promettrait la jouissance tranquille dans quelques-unes de nos colonies. Il faudrait en outre faire espérer aux condamnés la rémission de leurs peines, en récompense des services qu'ils auraient rendus à la patrie.

"Le premier noyau de ces hommes, au nombre d'environ deux mille, serait organisé en compagnies d'environ cinquante hommes chacune, qui auraient leurs officiers et seraient subordonnés à un chef unique chargé de l'ensemble des opérations. Ce chef serait investi d'une très-grande autorité.

. . . . .

"Il ne faut pas perdre de vue qu'une expédition tentée d'abord avec aussi peu de monde ne peut réussir que par des moyens extraordinaires.

"Il ne faut point de grands approvisionnements en effets d'habillement : les ressources de la troupe seront dans son courage et dans ses armes.

. . . . .

"Il faut que le débarquement se fasse sur plusieurs points de la côte, soit parce que la désolation et la terreur portées dans une grande étendue de terrain multiplieront aux yeux de nos ennemis la quantité de nos forces, soit parce que les moyens de subsistance en seront plus faciles.

" En arrivant, les chefs s'annonceront, eux et leurs soldats, comme *vengeurs de la liberté et ennemis des tyrans.*

. . . . .

" Il faut que la troupe jure *guerre aux châteaux* et *paix aux chaumières,* et que sa conduite, surtout au début, soit conforme à cette déclaration.

" A mesure qu'ils avanceront, ils ouvriront les prisons, recruteront les détenus, les incorporeront : ils appelleront les ouvriers, les indigents, les mécontents, à faire cause commune avec eux, leur présenteront des armes, des subsistances ; leur offriront l'appât du butin. Ils briseront toutes les voitures.

. . . . .

" Il faut poursuivre l'ennemi à outrance quand il est battu, et ne point faire quartier aux prisonniers.

"Il faut rompre les ponts, couper les communications, arrêter et piller les voitures publiques, brûler tout ce qui appartient à la marine . . . sommer les communes de rendre leurs armes ; exécuter militairement celles qui resisteraient."

Mr. Laws has kindly shown me an "Authentic Copy of the Instructions given by General Hoche to the American officer, Colonel Tate, who commanded the men employed in the French Invasion of South Wales in 1797." It commences thus :—

"There will be placed under the command of Colonel Tate a body of troops completely organised to the number of one thousand and fifty, all resolute, determined men, with whom he may undertake anything. They are to be called 'La Seconde Légion des Francs.'

"The legion is completely armed; he will

be likewise furnished with fast-going vessels with which he is to proceed before, with, or after the squadron; the vessels will be victualled for the passage, but the legion will bring on shore nothing but their ammunition, which is to be musquet cartridges.

"Colonel Tate is to have command in chief of the legion; the Admiral will give the necessary orders to the officer commanding the naval force, which will proceed up St. George's Channel, and the landing is to be effected, if possible, in or near Cardigan Bay."

The instructions then give directions that the expedition should make a feint of landing in Somersetshire, as was afterwards done; and the most minute and careful suggestions are made on the primary object of securing the co-operation of the Welsh people— General Hoche remarks that the poor are the most easy to rouse, as hunger makes people discontented. His followers, however, hardly carried out this truism in the way he intended; they devoured everything they could lay their hands on, and certainly succeeded in rousing the peasantry, but not exactly to co-operation. The loyalty of the people must have been an unpleasant surprise to the framers of the expedition.

It appears from the directions that two other legions were to have simultaneously invaded the counties of Northumberland, Durham, and York; these latter, however, never put in an appearance. The primary object to be attained by the Second Legion was the destruction of Bristol and Liverpool. On reaching Severn Sea should the former prove impracticable, then the legion was to land in Cardigan Bay, and march through Wales to Chester and Liverpool.

These instructions are taken from a pamphlet printed for J. Wright, 169, Piccadilly (1798), the text of which is copied from attested transcripts of the original documents. The instructions continue:—

"The expedition under the command of Colonel Tate has in view three principal objects. The first is, if possible, to raise an insurrection in the country. The second is to interrupt and embarrass the commerce of the enemy. The third is to prepare and facilitate the way for a descent by distracting the attention of the English Government." [1]

There is no doubt that the frigates did go up the Channel as far as Ilfracombe, causing consternation among the small craft, and great excitement on shore. They proceeded as far as Ilfracombe, where they scuttled some merchantmen. A letter is extant written by the town authorities to the Home Secretary. The volunteer regiments were

[1] Laws, "Little England beyond Wales." Mason, Tenby.

INTRODUCTION.

on the alert, and a considerable force was quickly mustered, which was possibly the reason that the French did not land in Somersetshire, but returning down the Channel made without any delay for the north coast of Pembrokeshire.

As has been seen, the local regiments here were no less brisk than their Somersetshire fellows. The Castle Martin Yeomanry Cavalry now carry "Fishguard" on their standard as well as upon the sabretaches of the officers, and upon the pouches of the troopers, a distinction granted to them in 1853, when the following letter was written by Lord Palmerston to Sir John Owen.

"WHITEHALL, *May* 18, 1853.

"SIR,—I have had the honour to lay before the Queen the memorial of the officers, non-commissioned officers, and privates of the Castle Martin Yeomanry Cavalry (which you transmitted to me), and I have the satisfaction to inform you that Her Majesty is graciously pleased to approve of the corps bearing the word 'Fishguard' on their standard and appointments.

"I have the honour to be, sir,
"Your obedient servant,
"PALMERSTON.
"Sir John Owen, Bart., M.P."

It is satisfactory to state that the Castle Martin Yeomanry Cavalry still maintains its reputation for efficiency and smartness, its team of ten men having won the inter-regimental challenge cup, and proved themselves the best shots among the forty competing yeomanry regiments in 1890, Corporal Williams, of St. Florence, having made the highest score of any yeoman in the kingdom. Thus giving us—the inhabitants of Pembrokeshire—the satisfactory assurance that, should invaders land on our coast now, they would meet with at least as warm a reception as they did a hundred years ago. And this suggests the idea that, in this age of centenaries, this strange occurrence should not be forgotten, but that in 1897 the landing of the French at Fishguard should be duly celebrated.

WEDNESDAY.

THE FIRST DAY.

THE FRENCH FRIGATES.
(From an old Print.)

THE FISHGUARD INVASION BY THE FRENCH IN 1797.

CHAPTER I.

THREE FRIGATES.

In the year of our Lord, 1797, there was a right fair day in February. The day was a Wednesday, the twenty-second of the month, and it was indeed the most pleasant day for that harsh season of the year that I can call to mind on looking back through the course of a long life. But it was not only the unusual beauty of it that made that Wednesday in February a day of mark, or I might scarcely have kept it stored in a corner of my mind for seventy years well-nigh—remarkable as fine days are in this climate that is chiefly renowned for fine rain ; but for the reason that this particular Wednesday was a day of utmost astonishment to all the dwellers on this North Pembrokeshire coast, and (I may venture to add) a day of much consternation to most of them.

A day still remembered by old Welsh fishwives, and still used by them as a means of terror wherewith to hush to sleep unquiet grandbabes, or to stir to patriotism stout but supine grandsons.

I was, at the time of which I speak, but a youth of fifteen, as thoughtless and careless as most lads of that age ; not very sensible to danger, save when it presented itself face to face with me at no more than arm's length, under which circumstances candour compels me to own I did not always enjoy it. I trust that I may say without undue boasting that

I did not fear anything greatly as long as it was out of sight, for which reason I have often thought that had I been born a generation or two later, and had I selected a soldier's career instead of that of a divine I might have fought excellently at a distance of a few miles from the enemy : though at close quarters I will admit that any unexpected danger might perchance produce a sense of amazement which the uncharitable might set down to faint-heartedness.

But that my nephews, nieces, and neighbours generally may know the truth concerning this matter—the landing of the French at Fishguard in 1797, I, Daniel Rowlands, clerk, being aged, but still of sound mind, have written this narrative—which when duly set forth will, I hope, convince the most sceptical as to the sort of spirit which animated my countrymen (if not myself), and still more my countrywomen.

On this fair morning then, at about ten o'clock, when I ought to have been pursuing my studies under the fostering care of one of the clergy at St. David's, I was in reality strolling along the headland of that name, led astray by the beauty of the day, which seemed too fair for book-lore; I was strolling along, doing nothing, thinking of nothing, wishing for nothing, yet, having found for the nonce the secret of true happiness, when I perceived a man on horseback approaching me at a furious rate. In spite of the pace at which he was advancing I recognised him as a servant of Trelethin.

"Whither so fast, John?" I shouted, in our own tongue. He was past me as I spoke.

"The French, the French!" came back to me on the breeze mingled with the sound of his horses' rushing hoofs. His voice or my ears failed, for I heard no more save—when the thunder of the hoofs had ceased, the duller but more continuous thunder of the waves rolling in freshly at the foot of the rocks.

John's words had left me much astonished. I knew—from my studies under the divine above referred to—that the French lived in France, where some of them had lately been engaged in beheading the rest with the help of a newly discovered machine. So much I knew, but why John Trelethin should yell "French" at me as he passed, riding apparently for his life, I knew not. What were the French to him or to me? As I advanced pondering the matter—but in a purely impersonal manner, and without any keen interest—at a little distance further along the cliff I espied the owner of Trelethin, John's master, standing very firm on his legs against a background of bright sea, his head inclining somewhat backward, while with both his raised-up hands he clutched a long spy glass, the small end whereof was applied to his eye. Following the direction of his spy-glass, I perceived a yet more astounding sight—astounding to us used to the world of lonely waters that lay stretched out in front of our homes. Three ships of war were passing slowly along our coast not far from land, they were accompanied by a smaller craft, which Mr. Williams informed me was a lugger. As he had been a sailor I took his word for it—but it did not make things clearer. What did it all mean? What did those vessels—or their inhabitants want here? They carried the English colours, I saw that for myself when Mr. Williams obligingly lent me the instrument.

"Take a look for yourself, my boy," he said—he was a man singularly free from pride—"Take a look at the blessed Frenchmen." (He did not say exactly blessed, but out of respect to my cloth I subdue his expressions slightly.)

"Frenchmen!" I cried. Then those were the French in those three vessels. I did not count the lugger, not being sure of her. Strange to say the first thought that flitted through my brain was one of pure joy ; here was an excuse, real, tangible, and startling, for having shirked my studies. With a little help from imagination (his and mine, which might act on each other as flint on steel, for he was an excitable man), I trusted I might so alarm my clerical guide and master as to make him quite forget the fact that I had given to St. David's Head the time I should have given to my own. The excuse might be made effective even should they prove to be not quite really French.

"They've English colours, sir," I said to Mr. Williams.

"Foreigners are deceitful," says he, "up

to any tricks. I can see the scoundrels swarming on the decks." (For by this time he again had applied the spy-glass.) "Ah!" he continued, handing the glass to his wife who had joined us, "If it was but night now and a bit stormy, we might put out a false light or two and bring them on the rocks in no time."

This was the moment afterwards immortalised by a local bard in these words—

> "Mrs. Williams Trelethin was know every tide
> From England to Greenland without guide.
> Mrs. Williams Trelethin was take the spy-glass,
> And then she cry out—There they wass!"

The three tall ships sailed on calmly, with the clear shining of the sea around them, dark objects in all that flood of light. They went northward—along our Pembrokeshire coast, where (had Providence so willed it) they might have made shipwreck on the sharp rocks anywhere. However the day was too fair to admit of any such hope.

The alarm spread quickly; men and boys came bounding over the gorse in every direction; even the women, with the curiosity of their sex, came forth from their homesteads, leaving the cawl[1] and the children to mind themselves, while their natural caretakers gaped open-mouthed at the tall ships filled with untold dangers.

The crowd on the cliffs followed in the direction of the ships, keeping them ever in sight. Helter-skelter we ran along, crossing deep gullies, then along bare headlands covered only with gorse and large grey stones, then passing under a great mass of rock, like to some gaunt castle or fort (but alas, lacking cannon), then, at rare intervals, where a stream ran into the sea, we would dip suddenly into a smiling little valley filled

[1] Cawl—leek broth.

with trees and bushes. But the stones and crags prevailed greatly over the softer scenes. I had now entered so fully into the spirit of this race that all thought of my studies passed away; the fear of the dominee was merged in the far greater fear of the French. And yet it was not wholly fear that possessed me, but a sort of tremor of excitement, and curiosity as to what might happen next. Noon passed, but none stopped for food—nor even (till we came to a village) for a Welshman's comfort in perplexity—a glass of cwrw da.[1]

At two o'clock, for no apparent reason, the Frenchmen came to anchor. This was opposite to a rocky headland called Carn Gwastad, which forms a portion of Fishguard Bay, some distance to the west of the town of that name, and, by reason of an intervening headland, quite invisible from it, and

[1] Cwrw da—good ale.

in truth from most other places. We had now come from St. David's Head, a distance of full ten miles, and I, for one, was glad to sit down on a gorse-bush and meditate a little as to what all these things might mean and where they were like to end, which I hardly dared to hope might somehow take the form of a bit of dinner for myself. To stay hunger I composed my mind for a nap while I reflected dreamily that my elders were taking more definite steps for the defence of their country; and the knowledge of this was gratifying to me.

CHAPTER II.

THE LANDING.

BESIDES Mr. Williams' John, who had been despatched at full speed to St. David's to rouse the inhabitants, another man was sent to give the news to the Lord-Lieutenant of the county, while others wended their way to various points on the range of mountains which divides Pembrokeshire into two parts; the result of their mission being apparent when night fell and beacons flared along the line of heights from Vrenny Vawr to Carn Englyn—the mountain of the angels, so named from the angel-visits received by a pious hermit who dwelt

CARREGWASTAD.

thereon, and who probably lacked more ordinary society.

Many other messengers were sent in various directions, but though in this way persons at a distance were warned of danger, many of those who dwelt close by were as yet insensible of it. Chiefest of these was the owner of the old manor house, Trehowel, situated just above the bay where the ships were lying-to—of which house we shall hear more anon. Mr. Mortimer was of a generous and confiding disposition —and, as a bishop should be, he was in truth—much given to hospitality. He was, moreover, about to celebrate the marriage of his son, and he had made ample provision of cakes and ale, not to mention meats and spirits for this purpose. The wedding was to be on the following day (Thursday, the 23rd of February, to be exact); the new daughter-in-law was much to his mind, and therefore heart and hand were even more lavish than usual, when, looking out seaward from amidst the bridal greenery, his spirit was stirred within him by the sight of the British flag.

Nothing would serve this hospitable gentleman but that the English officers should partake of his good cheer; so his orders flew forth in every direction—compliments and invitations to the officers, and directions to the servants as to the setting forth of a sumptuous repast.

In the meantime one of the great ships, heaving anchor, had quietly slipped round the corner—by which I would say, rounded the next headland, Pen Anglas, in an undemonstrative manner. Thus coming in sight of the men occupying the fort near Fishguard; these fired as in duty and fair observance bound—a salute to the flag that had braved a thousand years, and had never in all that considerable period of time been put to a viler use than the present, when—hey presto! down came the British colours with a run, and up flew the tricolour in its stead—the red, white, and blue colours of the Republic of the French.

The astonishment of those men in the fort at this unexpected transformation-scene must have been akin to an electric shock such as may be produced on the unwary by the careless placing of a hand on a magnetic eel. They had been completely deceived by the mock flag, and were more unprepared for the change than those men who had already scrutinised the three frigates with very doubtful eyes as they made their way along the coast of Pembrokeshire.

All disguise was now over; the enemy showed under their true colours at last, and convinced even the most liberal-minded (including Mr. Mortimer) that they were not English. Though truly if they had desired to appear under their most appropriate colour they should have sailed under the black flag of piracy, for the men on board these frigates were little better than freebooters. Many of the older persons present were minded to take them for a new and enlarged edition of the *Black Prince*—a pirate ship which had eighteen years previously brought his broadside to bear on the town of Fishguard, and kept up an animated fire all day with his six-pounders. However, he caught a Tartar—the master of a smuggling craft, who returned the fire with such goodwill, aided by clever hands and a cannon at the edge of the cliffs, that the *Black Prince* sheered off. "Set a thief to catch a thief;" but it were ungrateful to think on that proverb.

THE LANDING.

It was this circumstance which caused the fort at Fishguard to be erected, one of whose nine-pounders had just, in courtesy, saluted the frigate, who, not caring to face the other seven guns of the fort in anger, turned round speedily, and rejoined her companions at Carn Gwastad Point without loss of time.

On her way she intercepted a sloop which had—perhaps out of curiosity, perhaps from some nobler motive—ventured too near; probably the master of the sloop had not expected this sudden rearward movement—anyway he found himself a prisoner, and his boat a prize. I had jumped up from my reclining position, and stood watching his fate with anxiety and awe, knowing him to be a friend (for I was a Fishguard boy, and intimate with all the varieties of seamen to be found there), but being, at that distance, unable to tell which friend.

All the other boats in the bay stood out to sea with all speed, scudding away with white sails stretched, reminding even a matter-of-fact boy who abhorred poetry, similes, and all such inventions of schoolmasters, suggesting even to me the sudden, outspread, white wings of a flock of ducks frightened by the unwelcome appearance, from round the corner, of a fox. They got away safe, but the captive sloop was towed in triumph by the frigate back to Carn Gwastad, where she found her sister ships were already disgorging their freight of soldiers.

The sun was setting as the first boats set down their load on British soil. There were not many spectators of this act (the only one of a like nature since 1066, as far as my knowledge—not very profound—of history went), the inhabitants of the district, when they perceived that the landing was

THE LANDING.

to be on their own coast, having dispersed as quickly as a swarm of ants amongst whom a foreign body is introduced—each one making with the utmost speed for his own home in order to retreat with his valuables (including his family) further into the interior. I, however, was but young, and concluded that my family, who lived in Fishguard, could very well take care of themselves; while it was possible that my father, who was a somewhat stern parent, might not even accept the (to me) absolute necessity of keeping an eye on the French as a valid excuse for departing from my studies at St. David's without leave from my master. I had a certain amount of fear of the French, I do not deny it; but it was as yet in the abstract, and was a very different thing from the absolute fear I had of my father when I caught him (and he caught me) in a bad mood. Besides, though I considered curiosity a childish and feminine quality, and as such infinitely beneath my dignity, still I must own I did feel a sort of craving desire to know what those people were going to do next. So, hidden in a gorse bush on a headland which commanded the creek, I watched the sun go down like a red ball into the sea, throwing a light as of blood on the muskets in the boats beneath me, making the dark figures that swarmed over the sides of the ships look darker and more grimy, lighting up the three-coloured flags that unfurled themselves to the night breeze. Then there came a long path of crimson right across the grey sea, which, dying out as the sun set, showed that this fair day was gone—a day too fair and sweet to be the setting for foul deeds.

Suddenly there rose a shriek, or, rather, a succession of shrieks breaking through the twilight quiet, and a young woman shot out like an arrow from the back door of Trehowel, darted past me without pausing to answer a question, and, shrieking all the time, fled away into the interior, clutching tightly in her hand a foaming jug of beer. I heard afterwards that she ran on for miles, still clutching that jug of beer, which she had been drawing for the (supposed) English officers; when at last her master had awakened to the fact that the French were actually at his doors. She ran thus for miles, not even stopping to drink the beer.

She was shortly after followed by Mr. Mortimer himself, who came across the courtyard laughing in spite of the seriousness of the occasion, for he must needs smile at a joke. He spied me, for indeed I had jumped up to question Sally, and he came towards me.

"The poor maid has had a scare," said

he, with a twinkle still in his eye. "But, in truth, Dan, my boy, I suppose it is time to be off."

"Oh, there's a pity," said I; "about Master Mortimer's wedding—and all the meats and drinks!"

"Well, yes, I never meant them for the parley-vous," said he, mounting his horse which one of his farm-boys had brought out; "but I dare say they'll enjoy them all the same—they won't be wasted."

He turned in the saddle to give a last look at his old house, standing dark against a yellow-green twilight sky, pranked out with all the mockery of boughs and flowery arches. The trees in the courtyard had not yet put forth their leaves, but branches of myrtles and ever-blooming gorse and great bunches of primroses had made the place gay. Mr. Mortimer's face changed as he looked; he made no movement with the reins; he was very loath to leave his home. In his mind's eye he was viewing the heap of smoking ruins he might see when next he came, and he seemed to be resolving to meet fate and the French on his own threshold, when a woman's quick step came out of the now-deserted house.

"Oh, master," she cried, running up to us, "ar'n't you off yet! Quick, there isn't a minute; they are coming up the hill. For the young master's sake," she whispered. "Remember, you have got the money and the papers. Quick!"

He nodded, then shaking his rein, rode off without a word.

"And what are you going to do, Nancy?" said I. "Isn't it time for you to be off too?"

"Oh, no odds about me. I'll slip off somehow, but I must get the silver spoons first."

Then she turned from me, and her voice broke suddenly.

"Wherever is Davy — oh, wherever is he?" she sobbed.

"Cheer up, Nancy, my maid," said I, being well acquainted with her, and only ten years younger — an inequality made up for by my superior station and parts. "Wherever Davy is he's in mischief—that you may take your davy of; but he always comes out of it somehow."

I hope the reader will pardon this expression, but I was not at this time even a curate—being but fifteen—and the chance of my ever attaining that station seemed but remote.

At this moment the clang of arms and the sound of high-pitched voices broke on our ears.

"I'll have those spoons if I die for it!" exclaimed Ann, who was not much given to the melting mood. "Run, Dan, make for Fishguard as fast as you can." And without another word or a sign of personal fear, Ann George disappeared into the house.

I will not deny now, after the lapse of so many years, that my heart at this moment beat unpleasantly fast. I had already watched the landing of some of the French troops, but from a considerable distance, and there had been something unreal about the scene, something like to play-acting, or a dream; but now that I actually heard their voices, the effect was very different. They were really here, close by; there was no mistake about it. I had an almost overwhelming desire to take to my heels and run for it, but in spite of a very real fear, two feelings restrained me—one was a hesitation on account of Nancy, whom it seemed mean to desert;

the other was that curiosity to which I have already alluded, and which powerfully possesses most of the inhabitants of these regions, but more especially the females. The twilight was rapidly sinking into darkness as I crouched lower among the bushes and peered out with eyes which doubtless resembled those of a frightened bird. Never hare in its form felt more of a flutter at the heart than I experienced as those screeching, and yet savage, voices drew nearer and nearer. I did not understand French, but if I had I trust I should not have understood the nature of the expressions those men were using. It must be remembered that at that time we were accustomed to think of a Frenchman as of a two-legged tiger—which we spelt with a y—and then perhaps the horror that thrilled me may be understood. Suddenly the vague terror was turned into reality, as between me and the dusky sky loomed forth a wild figure, then another and another, then a confused crowd.

I could stand no more. With one bound I passed from behind my bushes in through the back door of the house—

"Nancy, hang those spoons!" I spoke in Welsh, and I fear my expression was still more forcible. "Come this minute, I'll wait no longer."

"Why, who asked you to wait?" said Ann George, ungratefully. "I thought you'd be half-way to Goodwick ere this."

At this moment her speech was interrupted by a sound as of thunder at the front door, while the parlour window came flying into the room before the butt-ends of French muskets. Even Ann George thought it now high time to take her leave.

So we departed as quickly and as silently as possible through the back door, while the front door was being shivered to atoms, and the enemy was pouring into the house over its remains. Quickly, indeed, we went now and the falling night favoured us; the enemy's own noise too rendered the slight addition of our footfalls totally unobservable. All the space between Trehowel and the cliffs swarmed with Frenchmen, and the uproar was bewildering.

"They'll make short work with your master's ale, Nan," I gasped, as we ran along under the cover of the earthen banks topped with gorse.

"Aye, and of the wine and the spirits, and of all the poor young master's wedding feast. Oh, indeed, I wish I had known they were coming when I was baking those pies and brewing that ale!"

I did not waste my breath by inquiring the reason of this aspiration, for the hill was rather heavy on my lungs, and her meaning was obvious. In a very short time we had reached Brestgarn, the abode of a worthy divine, the Rev. David Bowen, whom we found about to depart hurriedly, he having been no quicker to hear the alarming tidings than his neighbour at Trehowel; but, having heard it, he and his family were off for the interior as fast as horses and fright could take them. Only one of his servants, a man named Llewelyn, volunteered to stay behind, to keep, as far as in him lay, an eye upon his master's place and goods.

"Let us go to the top of Carnunda," suggested this man. "We can see everything from there."

Carnunda is a rock situated just above most things in this region; more especially just under it lies the tiny village and church of Llanunda — Unda being manifestly a saint, though I cannot truthfully say I ever heard anything about him—or her.

We got up to the top of this carn then, and there snugly ensconsed between huge boulders of stone—the place is large enough to hold six or seven hundred men, well protected by natural rock-work—we gazed on the scenes all around us.

First at the creek beneath us. It was now pitch dark—for the night was as black as the day had been bright—but the three tall ships of war were lighted up with cressets of fire; the lugger was there and the captured sloop, and the sea around them was alive with boats, still conveying troops to the land. The torches that they carried were reflected on the waves, elsewhere inky black—but here bearing long broken lines of light. Dark figures swarmed at the landing place, if so one could call, what was merely some flat slabs of rock; and all up the cliffs we saw ant-like beings crawling, and even (by the aid of a little imagination) we could fancy we heard their strong exclamations at the steepness of the path—made even steeper to them by the nature of their occupation, for they were rolling casks (evidently heavy) of gunpowder from where the boats landed them up to the top of the cliff. Some of these dark figures carried torches which shed a fierce glow for a small space through the black night. As we looked, one of the casks which had been by much effort shoved up to well-nigh the top of the cliffs, suddenly slipped from the Frenchmen's hands and rolled rapidly down the declivity—the roll speedily becoming a succession of jumps and plunges, till with a wild leap the cask fled over a final precipice and disappeared in the sea.

"Thank the Lord for that," said Llewelyn.

Nancy and I laughed aloud. It is impossible to give any idea of the exultation that we felt.

"What words they are using over that!" said Nancy.

"Oh, don't I wish we were near enough to hear them!" said I, totally unmindful of my future profession.

But shortly after we had even greater cause of rejoicing. The enemy (as we had already learnt to call them) were disembarking their cannon, and lowering these unwieldly articles of war into a long boat, but zeal outstripping discretion, they so overweighted the boat, that lurching forward heavily she upset, and the whole of her cumbrous cargo was shortly at the bottom of the sea. It was a satisfaction even to think of it. Aye, and we may think of it still, for to this very day those foreign cannon are rolling about and rusting in the unquiet waters of Carrig Gwastad creek—a proof, should one ever be needed, of the truth of this strange story.

"Thank the Lord again," said Llewelyn.

COTTAGE AT CASTELL.

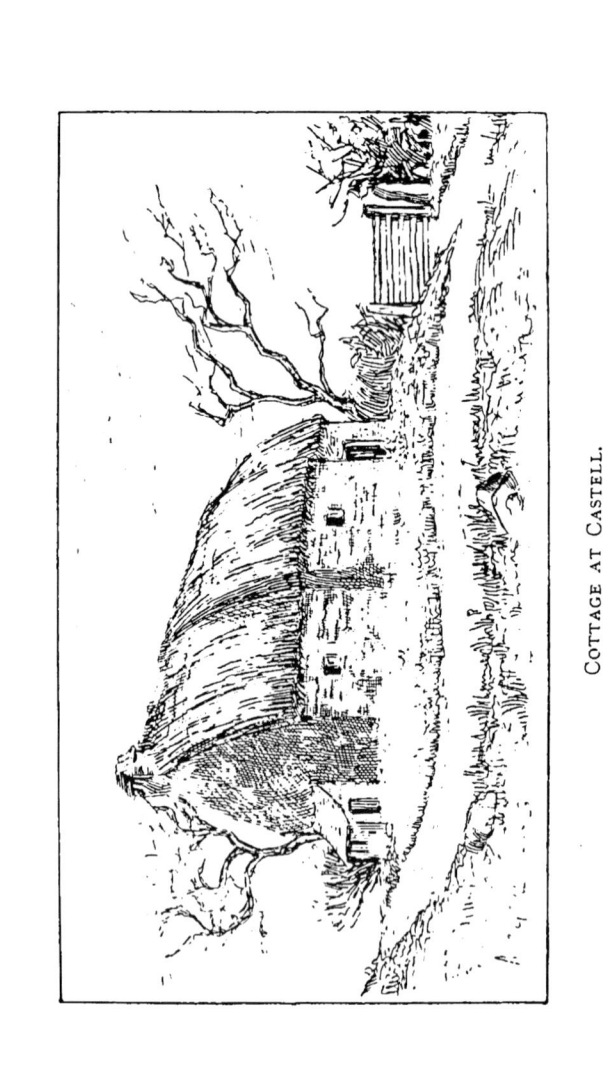

CHAPTER III.

THE FATE OF THE CLOCK.

GREAT bonfires now lit up the side of the hill beneath Trehowel—in the place still called the French camp—and scores of dark figures rushed about with torches flaring wildly in their hands; the whole scene reminding one forcibly of Pandemonium, that is, if one is capable of being reminded of a place one has never seen and that one has no desire to see.

Even the thought of it at the moment was unpleasant to me as bringing my neglected studies to my mind, so I hastily turned my attention once more to the French.

The boats and the sailors had now returned to their ships, having landed the invading hordes (which was the term we usually applied to the Gallic soldiers), who now seemed more bent on cooking than on conquering, on supping than on surprising. We watched the erection of beams and bars over the huge fires; and the slinging on to the bars of great pots and pans of all sorts—mostly intimate friends of poor Nancy who watched all these proceedings with many a groan and warm ejaculation as she thought of all her wasted scrubbings in the back kitchen of Trehowel. The precise number of the men who landed that night on a bit (though remote) of Great Britain was fourteen hundred; of whom six hundred were regular troops, and eight hundred were convicts of the basest sort, described, indeed, in the pamphlets of the time as the sweepings of the gaols. Besides these, there were two women; and had the fourteen hundred been animated by the spirit which possessed these two of the weaker sex, the result might have been much more unpleasant to the Principality than it actually was.

The Welsh woman beside me was not by any means deficient in spirit either, it even sometimes took the form of temper, yet to my astonishment I heard the sound of sobs which could only proceed from her, as Llewelyn was hardly likely to relieve his feelings in this way.

"Oh, Master Dan, wherever is Davy?" she again asked. She called me "master" when she remembered what I was going to be, otherwise my father being only a small tradesman in Fishguard, I was more frequently called Dan. I do not think I have given any description of Ann George, boys do not, as a rule, think much of personal appearance; nor did I. My idea of Nancy had been chiefly connected with the peppermints she had been in the habit of giving me as a child; I thought her a person of a free and generous disposition. She was a tall, fine young woman of five and twenty, with dark hair and eyes (these last being dark grey not brown), decided but pretty eyebrows, a well-shaped nose, and rather large mouth which disclosed when she laughed or talked (which was frequently) handsome white teeth. In short, she was the type of a good-looking Welsh woman. She had also a healthy colour, a warm heart, and a splendid appetite. It was not very surprising that she had (or had had) two admirers.

I at once referred to this fact with a boy's utter want of delicacy in matters of sentiment.

"What are you bothering about Davy for? I thought it was Jim you liked."

"Don't you ever say that fellow's name to me again, Dan'el," said Nancy with animation, her tears dried up and her eyes sparkling. "I hope never to hear of James Bowen again so long as I live."

I whistled. "Was that because he got into trouble for horse-stealing? Why, as to that, Davy's none too particular."

"Dear anwyl, Dan, talk of what you understand, or hold your tongue! What do I care for their customs and laws? 'Deed to goodness, nothing at all. As to James Bowen if it had been only that—but there, a child like you can't understand things."

"Can't I!" I shouted, thoroughly incensed—of course we spoke in Welsh, and used a good many more exclamations than I have set down here. "Can't I, indeed. I only know smuggling is——"

"Don't quarrel, children," said Llewelyn, who was of a quiet disposition. "And don't shout or you'll bring the French upon us. Silence holds it here.[1] Just look there!"

He pointed towards the opposite direction to that in which we had been looking, and where the French were still clambering about the cliffs dragging up the last of their barrels of ammunition and brandy. He pointed towards the steep road which leads from Goodwick to Fishguard. This road was thronged with people, horses, carts, furniture, cattle all mixed together, and all (the animate ones at least) making their way with such speed as their legs and the hill permitted away from the immediate neighbourhood of the invaders. The lights which some of them carried, and the glare from some gorse which had been set on fire, lit up the straggling, toiling multitude.

Further off the semi-circle of hills blazed with warning beacons. It was a sight

[1] "Taws pia hi," a Welsh proverb.

never to be forgotten; a sight that had not been seen in this island for centuries. From our high nest in the rocks we had but to turn our heads to see all. In front of us to the north stretched the sea; a little to the north-west was the creek where the French had landed, where we could dimly discern the tall masts of the war-ships lighted up fitfully by cressets of fire. At the top of the cliff was Trehowel, and close by was the French camp surmounted by the tricolor flag. A little nearer us was Brestgarn, where Llewelyn lived, and just at our feet was the village and church of Llanunda. Goodwick lay to the east of us; there was a steep hill down to it, a magnificent flat of sands, with sea on one side and marsh on the other, and then a steep hill up from it leading ere long to Fishguard. The sea came round the corner from the north in order to form that deep and beautiful

Goodwick Bay, where trees and rocks, gardens and wild waves, luxuriant vegetation and marshy barrenness are so strangely mixed. Behind all, to the south and southeast came the mountains; and towards the fastnesses therein most of these fugitives were wending their way.

"Deuks!" said Llewelyn, "they are coming out to see what they can get, the scoundrels; I must run back to Brestgarn."

"Let me come," said I, on the impulse of the moment—though my knees shook as I saw small dark clumps of men leaving the main mass and coming towards us; but Llewelyn inspired confidence, and curiosity has a courage of its own; then I suddenly bethought me of Ann George.

"But what will you do, Nancy?" I asked.

"I will go to my Aunt Jemima, I'll be safe enough with her; don't trouble about me, my dear," said Nancy, our short-lived quarrel being happily over.

"That is in Fishguard, you can't go there alone, wait a bit for me," said I, with youthful assurance.

"I can hide you at Brestgarn if you want to come, but better go on to Fishguard," said Llewelyn.

By this time, however, we were almost at the farm, for we had run down the steep side of Carnunda without any delay.

As we drew near to the house we found from the uproar therein that it was already full of Frenchmen. Very cautiously we approached a window and peeped in. We saw a strange sight. The kitchen was filled with ragged ruffianly fellows, all gesticulating with all their limbs, and screeching with all their lungs. Of course we did not understand a word they said, which, perhaps, was no loss under the circumstances. They were dressed in all sorts of uniforms—some of them in a dusky red (our soldiers' coats dyed, as I afterwards heard), others wore the regular dark blue of the French army. An enormous fire blazed on the hearth, on which they had placed a large brass pan, geese and fowls only half-feathered had been hastily thrown into it, and now they were literally cramming it with butter, which they dug out of a cask they had dragged in from the dairy. Suddenly a shout arose, apparently from the ground beneath us.

"Deuks!" said Llewelyn, again. "They've found the port."

Llewelyn did not allude to any of the harbours in the neighbourhood, but rather, it may be, to the lack of one, which had perhaps occasioned the wrecking of a vessel from Oporto laden with the wine of the district.

"No odds, don't fret for the wine,"

whispered Nancy. "We'll get plenty again. I only hope there's a good store of brandy in the houses, too."

We got our brandy in a different way, but also inexpensively, and there was at times a considerable stock of it, and tobacco, too, in the farmhouse cellars.

Llewelyn, however, was much perturbed: he had volunteered to stay to look after the household goods, and he didn't seem to be able to do much. The delight of the Frenchmen at such an unexpected treasure-trove was indeed exasperating. Down flowed the generous liquid through throats the outsides of which were much in want of shaving, elbows were raised, and voices also in the intervals of quaffing. Suddenly one man paused in his potations, the brass face of the old clock that stood in the corner had caught his eye, and the loud ticking of it had caught his ear. Screeching something that sounded like "enemy," he levelled his musket and fired straight at the clock. The bullet went through the wood-work with a loud sound of splitting.

" Brenhin mawr!" yelled Llewelyn, forgetting all caution in his exasperation. "The scoundrels have shot our eight day clock!"

Unfortunately his remark was overheard; and indeed his yell shot into the midst of those rioting ruffians like a pebble into a wasp's nest. Out they flew, evidently infuriated; but we waited for no explanations, taking to our heels on the instant, with the promptitude of extreme fear. Nan and I were light of heel, and favoured by the darkness—yet more black to those who came from that blaze of light—we got clear away; but turning ere long to look, we perceived that Llewelyn had not been so fortunate, he was older and a good deal heavier than we were; and then his righteous anger had rendered him rather breathless before he began to run. He was now surrounded by a crowd of foreigners, all jabbering and gesticulating as hard as possible. Our hearts were sore at having to leave our companion in this plight, but there was no help for it, to attempt a rescue would have been, under the circumstances, worse than folly. So we ran along across country, avoiding all roads, and making straight for Goodwick.

CHAPTER IV.

THE PRIEST'S PEEP-HOLE.

As Nancy and I puffed and panted in as noiseless a manner as possible up the steep hill from Brestgarn, we saw, or, more strictly speaking, we heard all around us, foraging parties of the enemy, who were making off with everything they could lay their hands upon. The screeching of poultry, the quacking of ducks, the cackling of geese, the grunting and squealing of pigs (I might go on as long as some foreign Delectus, but that I fear to weary the reader) together with the oaths and laughter of the Frenchmen, formed a medley of sound that might have been pleasing to the ears of a musician composing a symphony on rural sounds, but that to a more ordinary listener formed a hubbub of noise that was bewildering and extremely distasteful; while poor Nancy's vexation at the fate of the dwellers in the farm-yard equalled her indignation at the use made of her well-scrubbed pans.

Not a single inhabitant of this district seemed to be left, every cottage was deserted; all had fled for the present, in order to turn again with greater force and rend the intruder—as one may draw back for a space so as to gain the necessary impetus for a spring.

We had reached the village of Llanunda, when we heard a considerable body of the enemy marching along the road near us, on their way to take possession of our rocky nest on the top of Carnunda. This very strong position formed the enemy's outpost, and it ought to have been a matter of no small difficulty to oust them therefrom, had they but planted themselves firmly in it.

To our great dismay we now heard voices approaching us from the other side; these proved to be some of the foraging parties making themselves acquainted with the larders and cellars of all the neighbouring houses. We crouched down lower among the gorse bushes, and I at least knew precisely the sensations experienced by a hunted and hiding hare. When this danger, too, was happily overpast, at all events for the moment, Nancy whispered to me—

" Dan, they are a deal too near us here, and there's more coming. I know a better hiding-place than this. Let's make for the church."

I assented willingly; and we made as fast as we could for the church. It was a small but ancient building, full of queer holes and corners, with the which Nancy was better acquainted than I was, it being her parish church. The door was happily unfastened, but no Frenchmen had as yet invaded the sacred building, for we took the precaution of looking through the "leper's hole" as soon as we had entered the porch. The leper's hole is a little square window, the sides of which are so sloped as to command a view of the interior of the church, more especially of the chancel; so that in the old times even these miserable wretches—set apart in the porch—might still behold the high altar.

We then looked with eagerness through this orifice, and perceived gladly that the building was dark and empty. So pushing open the door, we entered our sanctuary as though it had been a veritable city of refuge. Our first care was to secure the door as well as we could on the inside; then Nancy sat down in order to fetch her breath, while I reviewed the place and the situation. Neither were to my mind when I came to think of it.

"What have you come here for, Nan?" I inquired. "I don't like it—we'll be caught here like rats in a trap. We can't hide in the pulpit. I'd rather a gorse-bush in the open, now."

"Wait a bit, Dan, till I fetch my breath—and don't talk; they may hear you," said Nancy, not considering that she was talking herself.

"Oh do make haste with your breath," said I, "and tell me where it is." I was full of curiosity to know where her hiding-place could be: the church was pitch dark, a few minutes of silence there seemed an age. "It's not in a vault, is it?" I continued.

"A vault—bless the boy—no! I'm not going into a vault before I can help it. Well, if you won't be quiet, I suppose I'd better show you the place. It is at the other side of the church. Come across quietly, now."

We did go across as quietly as we could, considering the pitch darkness of the place, all blocked up with high pews according to the fashion of the time. In my after-career I had often occasion to reprove the occupiers of like boxes, who, trusting to their wooden walls to screen them, slumbered happily within a few yards of me, utterly forgetful of the treachery of their own noses.

After having injured her shins several times over unexpected obstacles, Nancy sighed forth, "Oh for a light!"

"Oh for something to eat!" I responded. "I've got a flint and steel in my pocket; but I can't eat that. You can have it if you like."

"I daren't strike a light," said Nancy; "but I've got a bit of cheese in my pocket along with the silver spoons. Here, stretch out your hand."

"Don't you want it?" I felt impelled by manners to say this, though I felt wolfish.

"Not I. I had my dinner as usual. I put it in my pocket in case of meeting—a friend."

"Do your—friends like cheese?" I asked with my mouth full.

"You seem to, any way," retorted Nancy. "I hear them coming."

I bolted the cheese in a panic. I felt much more afraid of the French since I had seen them so near in Brestgarn kitchen, and since they had nabbed Llewelyn.

"Here's the hole—you go first. I'll close it up after us with a pew door."

Nancy dexterously lifted one off its hinges, while I, mounted on the back of a pew, groped my way into a pitch dark cavity in the wall, the entrance to which was situated at the height of some three or four feet above the floor-level.

"Take care, there are steps," said Nan, just as I had discovered the fact by the aid of my shin-bone. She was still wrestling with the pew door, and I smothered my agony chiefly, I must own, from fear of the French.

"Get on a bit higher up, Dan," whispered Ann, as she followed me, dragging the door after her as quietly as she could. Nancy was certainly a wonderful woman, with a head on her shoulders.

At this moment I felt that it was so, for I was propelled somewhat violently upward by the member in question. I can also add my testimony that she was a hard-headed woman. She was also perhaps a little hard-hearted, for in answer to my remonstrance, "Hold hard, Nancy, that hurts!" she merely said,

"Oh, do get on, Dan; I expect them here every minute."

I did get on, and found after mounting

half-a-dozen steps of a twirling stair, that my head was opposite an opening just at the place where the roof of the church sprung; one of the oaken beams was, in fact, a little scooped out to make room for this slit, which being under the heavy shadow of the woodwork was almost completely screened from the glances of those below; while to the person placed behind this coign of 'vantage the whole of the interior of the church was visible—chancel as well as nave.

"What a queer place—what's it for, Nancy?" I asked.

"That is called the Priest's Peep-hole; I suppose in old times he got a friend to go up there and keep an eye on the congregation— see who went to sleep, and what they were at altogether," explained Nan; but at this moment her eloquence came to a sudden end. Our voices and our hearts died within us, for there came to our ears the dreaded but expected sound—the clamorous jabber of many tongues.

The sounds came from the churchyard, but I doubt if even a company of good Welsh ghosts would have frightened us as much as these earthly foreigners. Very, very earthly and carnal-minded did they seem to us at this moment.

"They won't come into a church—they won't rob a church!" I whispered to Ann, leaning my head down close to her's—a difficult feat, but I was as thin as a lath then.

"Won't they?" said Ann, scornfully. "You wait a minute—Hst!"

Nan's appreciation of character and computation of time proved equally correct. She had fixed the pew-door by this time, and she held it firmly in its place by the handle, which she had taken care to put on the inward side when she lifted up the barrier across the entrance to the stair.

"I hope they won't fire through that like they did through the clock at Brestgarn, on the chance of finding some one behind it," I whispered to my companion as this comfortable idea flashed through my mind, even the terror of the French failing to curb my natural love of suggesting a terror.

"Hst!" retorted Nan; "hold your tongue, can't you, and keep your head down; don't let them see you peeping, Dan!"

Nancy's caution to me came not a moment too soon, for crash! a rush of men and muskets at the door, whose ricketty bolts we had drawn when we entered, chiefly in the hope that they might *not* be tried. But if we drew them as a sort of charm, the spell was not strong enough, nor were the locks.

C-r-a-ck—*crack!* the feeble bolts gave a groan, and open flew the door with a sharp, splitting sound. In rushed ten or a dozen Frenchmen, tumbling over one another in

THE PRIEST'S PEEP-HOLE.

their haste. The church was lighted up with a sudden blaze from their torches; this was all I saw, for on the entrance of the enemy I had ducked my head speedily. Ann could see still less, as she was crouched on the bottom step, and was keeping the door in its place with her knees.

The noise in the church was terrific, but yet to my ears the beating of my heart was still louder. The more I tried to silence it, the more it ticked.

"Perhaps they'll think it's a clock," I reflected.

"Oh, dear! oh, dear!"

Yet after a while, as I grew more accustomed to the clamour, I became possessed by a desire to know what these men were doing. Very cautiously I raised my head, I feared my hair must be standing on end, which would make it more perceptible by an inch or two. Instinct had made me take off my hat as we entered the building; in crossing the dark aisle I had dropped it, and I hoped sincerely no one would find it, as it might lead to unpleasant investigations. Planted finally on my hands and knees, I raised myself till my eyes were on a level with the lowest part of the priest's peep-hole, and then, even veiling my eyes with half-closed lids as a precaution, I glanced furtively forth at the foreign marauders beneath me. They had not gone through the ceremony of removing their hats, and their object in entering the sacred edifice was evidently simply the hope of plunder. With the butt ends of their muskets they knocked and thrust at everything, as if to ascertain of what it was made, and whether anything of value might not be concealed within it. One half-drunken fellow came and gave a mighty bang to the cushion belonging to the pulpit, which he snatched from its proper position and dashed against the wall, immediately under my spy-hole. I imagine that the worthy incumbent must have been less given to pulpit thumping than most of his fellows, for out flew a cloud of dust, reaching even to my nostrils. A smothered sneeze was the result. Instantly I felt myself violently pulled by the leg from below; indeed, so provoked was Nancy that she could not resist giving me a shake, though I am sure the candid reader will allow I was not to blame in the matter.

Unluckily the Frenchman had heard the sneeze, and some animated conversation went on between him and his companions, who, however, seemed inclined to ridicule his assertions. Judging from the tone of their remarks (for Nancy held too tight a grip of me to allow of my seeing anything), I should say that their language to each other was not so polite as one might have expected from men of their nation. However, my particular enemy did not seem inclined to allow himself to be set down after this fashion; for, dropping his cushion, he proceeded to make an investigation with his clubbed musket. Walls, pews, and benches, he thumped them all indiscriminately, giving a sounding whack to the door which closed our retreat. But Nancy's knees did not flinch, though they must have received a most unpleasant jar. Luckily the entrance to the hidden stair was in a very dark and out-of-the way corner, and also at a very unusual height from the ground. Mercifully at this moment our tormentor's attention was distracted by a shout from his comrades, who had entered the little vestry, and had forced open the cupboard containing the sacramental vessels. These were very ancient, and were of silver, and the glee of the finders was easily understood even by those in our retired situation.

Others of the invaders broke open the chest containing the parish records, but, much disappointed by the nature of the contents, they tore forth the documents and tossed them on the floor of the church. Human nature was no longer to be restrained, neither by fear nor by Ann, so I once more popped my head up and beheld a strange sight. One of the men had thrown a torch in among the parchments and papers, a bright flame lighted up the dark interior of the church, and shone on the fierce faces of the men around the fire, two of whom were struggling for the possession of the communion cup.

"Great Heaven, we shall be burnt like rats, Nan!" I whispered to my companion, but she answered by her favourite expression, " Hst !"

One soldier, I imagine by way of a joke, now threw the pulpit cushion on the flames, whereupon such dense clouds of smoke arose as speedily cleared the church of the invaders, but alas, nearly stifled us, the lawful inhabitants. Luckily the floor of the church was of slate, and the fire was not very near any woodwork.

Nancy insisted that we must bear our suffocation in silence and motionless, and though my eyes watered and my heart rebelled, not a cough nor a wheeze, nor even a word, did I suffer to escape me, but to my thoughts at least I gave free rein. After a while these too played the truant, wandering away from my enemies and dreamily fixing themselves on my master at St. David's, my school friends, my books, the moving waters that framed in every picture of my life, till, becoming more and more indistinct, I imagine that I must have fallen fast asleep, though this is a matter that none can speak of with any certainty till it comes to the sharp act of awakening, which act assures us, in the most matter-of-fact manner, that we have been asleep.

In this way, by a sharp fact, indeed, no other than Nancy's elbow, I made the discovery that, in spite of my uncomfortable position, I must have fallen sound asleep, tired out by my long walk and many subsequent runs, and fatigued also by the number of new ideas forced on my mind by the action of the extraordinary events of the day and the many bewildering things I had seen and heard since breakfast time that morning.

It seemed to me to have been but a few minutes from the time the French left us choking in the smoke till I felt that elbow of Nancy's, of which I took no notice. Indifferent to this silent scorn, she now pulled me vigorously by the leg.

"Wake up, Dan! Wake up, boy; we must

get away from here at once; we ought to have gone long ago, but I fell asleep, worse luck. Come now, at once, it's just daylight."

We had, indeed, quite suddenly, as it seemed to me, reached the morning of Thursday.

THURSDAY.

THE SECOND DAY.

A Ransacked Farmhouse.

CHAPTER V.

DAVY JONES' LOCKER.

THE fear of the French returning suddenly shook the drowsiness out of my eyes. I gave them a final rub, then stumbled down the crooked steps after Nancy. How she could have guessed that it was now near dawn—as in our corner it was still pitch-dark—was a mystery to me; but probably the habit of waking up daily at an extremely early hour, as was the wont of milk-maids in those days, had accustomed her to know the time to a nicety.

We crept as quietly as we could down from our uncomfortable hiding-place, so stiff and cramped that we could only move with difficulty, and every bone made its particular position known with great accuracy, even to us who were totally unacquainted with anatomy. Then we carefully reconnoitred our situation.

As far as we could see, looking through the church windows on every side, we gazed only into the dim dusk of early morning into a lifeless world. No little bird as yet sent up his morning song; there were no sheep or cattle to be seen, their lawful owners or the invaders having driven them off to securer quarters or to sudden death, as the case might be. The church itself, after the late uproar, seemed very silent now; the fire had quickly died down, smothered by the pillow; only the heavy smell of smoke remained to prove that the wild doings of the night had not been a terrifying dream.

We crept along to the leper's hole, using

the other end of it now ; for the unfortunate outcasts of former days had gazed through the tube into the church, while we unhappy fugitives looked warily from the interior into the porch, to see if haply some blue-coated soldier might have been left there on guard. But if this had been the case he had certainly declined to stay, which was not unlikely considering the lax discipline, or, rather, total want of discipline, which prevailed in the French force. At all events, the porch was empty.

So after a little getting behind each other and a slight backwardness in going forward, owing more to uncertainty of light than natural timidity, at last we ventured out boldly into the porch, and took a good look, our necks stretched out over the churchyard and round the country. The former seemed silent and deserted, the tombstones looming darkly into dim twilight, which still lay heavy on the land; nor could we even discern any sound of snoring. Carnunda was crowned with fires and thronged with soldiers, but it was not very near, and we thought we might slip away unnoticed. So, cautiously we closed the door behind us, and fared forth. The porch lay to the south of the church; we were stealing round the building to the north, or seaward side, as being further removed from Carnunda, when we were stopped by a sudden shout, proceeding apparently from the air above us. Our hearts stood still and our blood froze with terror—at least, I know mine did, and Nancy turned an ashy white in the grey dawn. In an instant we looked up to the place from which our enemy had spied us—the roof of the church, where he had been stationed as a sentinel. He sat astride on the ridge, which could be easily gained by means of a flight of steps, made on the outside of the roof, as a look-out place from which to signal to those at sea; but never designed for such a purpose as the present. The discipline had not been so lax as we hoped. For a moment we were stupefied, wishing only that one of the graves would open and take us in. Then we took to our heels. Down came the Frenchman clattering over the roof of the church, from the edge of which he dropped to the ground, only a distance of eight or nine feet; then he came full cry after us. His shouts had attracted the attention of a couple of his fellows, who were strolling along the cliffs in search of what they could devour, or, still better, drink. They joined the chase instantly, and all three came full tear after Nancy and myself, who had headed straight for the cliffs, as one of our own foxes would have done, though what we were to do when we gained them save plunge into the sea we knew not. However, we were not fated to gain them just at present, for one of the Frenchmen had outrun Nancy, whose limbs were still cramped, and who was weary from want of rest and sleep. I was stiff and tired too, but fear of the French made me fly, and would have done so I think had I been doubled up by rheumatism. However, though Nan was caught, and warned me of her disaster by a shrill scream, I am glad to say she preserved her usual Welsh spirit, as she plainly showed by fetching the Frenchman a sounding box on the ear. I hesitated what to do, divided between fear of the French and the desire of standing by my friend. I am glad to say I had advanced a few steps towards an attempt at rescue, when some dark body rushed past me in the dawning light, and ere I could even exclaim, the Frenchman lay flat on the ground. The other two, half drunk, and wholly stupefied, perceiving that things were going somewhat crookedly, departed as quickly as they could, making for the camp at Carnunda. Our rescuer had a mind to follow them, but Ann laid a restraining hand upon his arm.

"Oh, Dio bach,"[1] she said, "I am glad to see you this time, if I never was before."

And she really looked as if she could have kissed him.

"Nancy, how came you here; why didn't you go away with the rest?" asked Davy Jones, abruptly, his voice rough and angry. He had had too great a scare to be tender or even civil.

"Why, I had to stop and see to everything—and the silver spoons," said Nancy, quite meekly.

"Hang the silver spoons," said Davy. "Now what's to be done with this carcase?" And he pointed to the unconscious Frenchman. "Get out of the way, Nancy, and I'll shove him over the cliff."

[1] Dear Davy.

"No, no, don't waste time," exclaimed Nancy; "we'll have the whole lot after us in a minute; they're as thick as ants on Carnunda. How can we get away?"

"Down the cliff as fast as you can. I've got a boat down below; if we can get to the caves we'll do; but I had some of them after me a little while ago, and I landed here to get rid of them, and to find out what had become of you, for Llewelyn of Brestgarn told me you were somewhere near."

"Llewelyn is a prisoner; did you see him? Is he safe?" asked Nancy, as we hurried along.

"Hush, quick and quiet; I'll tell you in the boat," whispered Davy.

We plunged down through dry bracken, gorse bushes, and large boulders of stone, interspersed with steep pieces of cliff. We jumped, slid, and tumbled down, clutching hold of grasses and ferns to stay our speed, and in a few moments we had reached the level of the sea.

The boat had been so cunningly hidden—with the dexterity of constant practice—that Nan and I quite failed to discover it. Davy, however, had it out in a trice.

"Jump in, boy, and give a hand to Nancy."

Nancy did not require a hand, she jumped in very steadily, and took the rudder. Davy threw me one oar, took the other himself, and we were off, stealing noiselessly along under the great cliffs, where darkness still dwelt. But the sky over our heads grew lighter every moment, and we ruefully perceived that ere long it would be broad day. Yet it seemed safer to be on the water than on the land, where we could even now discern dim figures looking for us.

"Ah, what is that?" in a horror-struck whisper from Ann.

That was a dark blue object, very unpleasing to behold, sodden with water, and wedged in a crevice of the cliffs.

"That is one of them," said Davy, grimly, "cleft to the chin by a scythe in a Welshman's hands. The ruffians had burnt his cottage, with his old mother in it; he caught this one, that's all. I wish I had served that fellow up there the same, Nancy."

"Where have you been, Davy?" I asked, to divert his remorseful thoughts, and unable to restrain my curiosity.

"Among these blacks of parlez-vous. They nabbed me last night as neat as could be—we had a bit of a scrimmage though. I was coming back from a little bit of business."

"Oh, Davy, you shouldn't!" from Ann.

"And I got in too near, never expecting ships here; who would? We were round the corner and on them almost, before we knew it; we made off then, but they saw us and gave chase. We made as fast as we could for a place I know, a good out-of-the-way cave—we've got a few about here, Nan—and they came after us. They'd some man who knew the coast among them, that I'll swear; any stranger must have found out the sharpness of our rocks; but not a bit of it. On they came quite comfortable, and close behind us they were as we got to the mouth of the cave. Levi Mathias stood up in the bow of the boat ready to jump ashore when one of the French marines shot him. I hope to have something to say before that's done with yet. Out tumbled our men anyhow, running through the surf and up the cliffs, into the darkness anywhere, for the Frenchmen carried torches as well as muskets. Well, they nabbed me."

"You didn't like to leave Levi," said Nancy, softly.

"I didn't like to leave the brandy," said Davy. "They got it, though, and me, tight enough. It put them into a good temper, however, and they didn't shoot me through the head, like they did a farmer that they made help to roll up their casks of ammunition, when he tried to escape. They made me carry up one of my own kegs which went against the grain; then they took me to their chief."

"Did you see the chief?" I asked, eagerly.

"'Deed to goodness, yes—General Tate—no more a Frenchman than I am; Irish, I'm thinking. He seemed very uneasy, and none of his men minded him. I had company—John Owen, of the sloop *Britannia*, laden with culm for Llanstinan—they didn't care for culm, and were cross to him, and a mortal fright he was in, but had sense enough left to tell them a lot of lies.

Then I saw Llewelyn, and had a word on the sly with him; he told me you were hereabouts; I watched my chance, and an hour or two ago I slipped down over the cliffs, seized this boat, and made off; but they saw me from one of the ships, and gave chase, and——"

A cry interrupted him, succeeded by a loud splashing of oars.

"And, hang them, there they are again. Why-ever couldn't you hold your tongue, Dan?"

This was unjust, as Davy had done all the talking himself; but the present was no moment for arguing. We bent to the oars with a will and in silence, till my hands were blistered, my heart panting, and my back breaking, and still the enemy were gaining on us.

Nancy leant forward.

"Change with me for a spell, Dan. I can row."

On we went again, fast, faster, and still the other boat came on after us yet more rapidly—it was like a nightmare. We came in very close to the cliffs now, and Davy took both oars. In between two reefs of rocks we went—a deep channel, yet full of treacherous windings and turnings.

"I think we'll do now," said Davy. "Please Providence, they may easily be smashed to atoms here."

And he looked gratefully at the sharp rocks.

But I turned after a little, and beheld that phantom-like pursuer still following us closely through the windings of the passage. The reefs had now become high cliffs, and seemed to close us in on every side; but as we came round another corner we saw before us a low archway. Through this we shot, and we found ourselves as it were at the bottom of a tea-cup, with precipitous walls on every side; just in front of us a little sandy beach. Davy pushed the boat towards a narrow slit in the rocks.

"Jump in there, my girl," he said. "Don't be afraid; if you slip, I'll catch you."

Nancy jumped at once, I followed her, landing half in and half out of the water, but quickly drawing myself up to be out of Davy's way, who came with a mighty rush—at the same time spinning the boat to the other side of the creek—only just in time, the Frenchmen were in the archway.

"Go on as far as you can," whispered Davy. "If they see this slit, they can only come one at a time, and——"

He didn't finish, but it wasn't necessary. Nan and I stumbled on in the interior, and found ourselves ere long in quite a large cave, where even in the dusky light we could discern objects extremely like kegs, also bales and packages of all sorts. Outside we heard the cries and screams of the Frenchmen, baulked of their prey; for (probably fortunately for themselves) they did not discover the narrow and hidden entrance to our cave. We were soon joined by Davy, who remarked that if they had a guide with them, there were a few things he didn't know yet.

"There's plenty of food here—and spirits—if we want to stay," he continued; "but perhaps we may as well get to the top and see what is going on."

CHAPTER VI.

WELSH WIVES.

WE did prefer (as soon as we had got our breath again) knowing what was going on in our usual world overhead to remaining in ignoble security in Davy's locker, for so we named his cave. Accordingly we scrambled and crawled and pushed our way up the far-end of the cavern, till at last the aperture resembled a chimney lined with ferns instead of soot more than aught else. We emerged at last into the open air full of morning sunshine, and perceived that we were now quite beyond the enemy's lines and once more among our own people.

The first thing to be done in this situation

was naturally—to talk; as good and true Celts we all agreed to that; and when we got into the high-road we found no dearth of people to talk to. They were gathering like ants from every quarter, and the one topic which each man liked to discourse on was simply this: how he was going to fight the French. The bonfires last night had aroused the country, and some of the men we met had come from distant parts of the county.

Among other items of news they told us that the men of St. David's had rushed in a body to their cathedral, from the roof of which they had insisted on tearing off the lead; six blacksmiths had come forward, and had at once cast the said lead into bullets. Old and young, master and man, all had turned out. A dissenting minister was there (the Reverend Mr. Jones was his name), and after him marched all the men of his congregation. The news had come as he was preaching to them, and the worthy man had at once changed rhetoric for action. "Let us fight a good fight," said he, and proceeded to put his words to the proof and himself at the head of his men.

A choleric major rode about the lanes near St. Dogmael's collecting recruits. He met a Mr. Jones (another one) : "Come along to fight the French," was Major James' greeting. But Mr. Jones had business which called him elsewhere.

"By the Lord Harry," said the Major, drawing his sword, "if you don't come this minute I'll slice your head off like a turnip."

The fear of the French was an unknown quantity, but the fear of the Major was very well known indeed, and Mr. Jones went.

We mingled exultantly with the throng of our people, and presently our eyes were gladdened by the sight of a gallant body of men—all well equipped and well mounted—the Castle Martin Yeomanry. These were joined by the Cardiganshire Militia, the Fencible Infantry of Colonel Knox, and some seamen and artillery, the whole under the command of Lord Cawdor.

We had got into Fishguard by this time, and we hung about the door of the "Royal Oak," where a council of war was being held by our officers—namely, Lord Milford, Lord Cawdor, Colonel Knox, Colonel Colby, Colonel Ackland, Colonel Dan Vaughan, Major James, and the Governor of Fishguard Fort, Colonel George Vaughan. The troops formed in the turnpike road just outside the town, and here we three had to separate, for Davy wished to accompany the troops, Ann to join her Aunt Jemima, and I to get something to eat at my father's house, for I had only had hasty snatches hitherto, and I had a growing boy's appetite. My parent was so much astonished at the course of events that he was not even surprised to see me when I walked, as bold as brass, into his shop; and never even asked if I had taken French leave of my master. But before satisfying my natural filial affection I (together with Davy) escorted Nancy to the abode of her relative, who, however, was not at home. As we turned to go, Nancy having taken leave of Davy in an affectionate manner, because, as she said, he had appeared just in the nick of time, we espied that stalwart female, Jemima Nicholas, coming along the road from Goodwick surrounded by twelve Frenchmen,[1] whom she had had the courage and address to bring—probably allured by false promises—all the way from Llanunda; assisted by the military, she now conducted them into the guard-house at Fishguard.

[1] A fact.

Leaving Nancy under the efficient protection of her aunt with light hearts, Davy and I went our several ways ; but ere long, after recounting my adventures and receiving a large amount of hero-worship from my mother, I once more found myself on the road leading to the scene of action. It seemed impossible to keep away. On the top of a high rock I saw a crowd of people in a state of great and evident excitement. I hastened to join them, and perceived at once the reason of their gesticulations. There were the three tall men-of-war and the lugger, with all sail set, standing out from the land, and apparently sailing away with all speed to the place from whence they came. We could hardly believe our eyes. We looked at Carnunda ; there floated the French flag, and the rocks were dark with men.

"The Lord hath delivered them into our

hand," said the Reverend Mr. Jones, who stood near.

This sight increased the confidence of our people amazingly, as much as (we afterwards heard) it struck dismay into the hearts of General Tate and his men, they not being animated by the spirit which moved the classic heroes to burn their boats so as to destroy the means of retreat and to force themselves to action. The base desertion of their comrades, the large supply of brandy in the farm-house cellars, and a providential but comic mistake, seem to have been the three principal causes of the failure of the French—one may say of the utter and singular collapse of their undertaking.

The mistake occurred in this manner. Large numbers of the country-women (among whom were Jemima and Nancy) had assembled on a hill commanding an extensive prospect, including the French outpost at Carnunda, desiring, with the curiosity of their sex, to see as much as possible of what was going forward. It was, by the way, the same hill on which I had also stationed myself. Most of the women wore their distinctive shawl, a scarlet whittle, this being the colour appropriated by the daughters of Pembrokeshire; while their Cardiganshire neighbours have adopted the white whittle. All of them at that time wore high black hats. Lord Cawdor, as he was riding about inspecting things in general, was struck by the resemblance of a mass of these women to a body of regulars, and he called upon the daughters of Cambria to give a proof of their patriotism by marching towards the enemy in regular order. The females responded by a considerable cackle, which, however, signified assent. I saw Jemima and her niece in the front of the regiment which moved forward boldly towards the enemy. Ere long a sudden dip in the ground rendered them invisible to the French, at which place, turning into a side lane, they came again to the back of the hill whence they had started, and renewed their former course; it was done almost in the way in which, I am told, these effects are managed in a theatre. This manœuvre caused much laughter among the spectators, and no little puffing and panting to the fair sex who accomplished it, many of whom were somewhat stout and not very young. However, it had the desired effect. General Tate acknowledged afterwards that they had been taken for a regiment of regulars, and the French troops (greatly composed of convicts) utterly lost heart. If they had but realised that it took a matter of seven days for the news to travel to London, they need not have distressed themselves on the score of quick aid from England.

In the meantime parties of marauders in a half-drunken state continued to prowl about the neighbourhood. A considerable number of militia and peasantry encountered five of these men, who were dragging with them a young calf. They dropped the calf and advanced to the combat, while our men, thinking the odds unfair, singled out five of our sailors (of whom Davy Jones was one), and Mr. Whitesides, a Liverpool gentleman who assisted, as a stranger, at the selection, dismissed them to their work with this benediction:—

"Take time, my boys, and do it well!"

The French soldiers fired, and one of our men fell, wounded in the foot; then it was the tars' turn, and they fired with such judgment that three of the enemy lay flat on the ground, and the remaining two departed rapidly. One of the three proved to be dead, the other two badly wounded. This encounter of a few, with a multitude looking on, took one back to the old days of Arthur's knights, or to the still older days of Goliath of Gath.

Considerable numbers of Frenchmen were by this time in a very unpleasing state of body and mind in consequence of rash indulgence in port wine and poultry boiled in butter. They were captured in small groups by the peasantry, who laid in wait for them behind the gorse bushes which abound in this region, and who jumped out on them with scant ceremony whenever they had a chance. A man belonging to Llanunda village, taking a cautious peep through his own little window from the outside, perceived one of the enemy making free with his food and wine; the Frenchman was enjoying himself thoroughly, he had made an excellent fire from most of the furniture, and he was toasting his legs thereat as he sipped the generous wine with the air of a connoisseur. This was more than the Taffy could stand. He had not saved that wine from a wreck at considerable personal risk to see it sending a glow through the veins of a foreigner; he flung himself into the room with a strong expression behind his teeth and a hay-fork clenched tightly in his hand. The Frenchman jumped up and thrust with his bayonet at the master of the house, who turned aside the blow, then, taking the foe on his pitchfork, tossed him into the fire, as he might have pitched a truss of hay on to the rick.

A party of marauders set forth with the view of plundering Manorowen, a gentleman's seat in the vicinity; but being followed by a detachment of the Yeomanry, they returned in a very different manner from what they had anticipated.

And now we, on our knoll—and there

were some thousands of us, including peasantry, fishermen, shopkeepers, and the resident gentry of three counties—raised a shout of pride and triumph as Lord Cawdor at the head of his small troop of Yeomanry Cavalry rode off to inspect the enemy at close quarters. The sinking sun shone on their glittering accoutrements and splendid uniforms, and a glow of satisfaction filled our hearts as we noted the fine chargers they bestrode, for a Pembrokeshire man loves horseflesh as truly as a Yorkshire man; and not even my cloth has ever restrained me from being a genuine Philhippos. The Castle Martin Yeomanry have always been celebrated for their horses; and indeed it was no matter of surprise to any one to hear, as we did hear afterwards, that General Tate mistook these men for the staff surrounding some English general, the main body of whose troops were defiling around the side of the mountain; in truth, as the courteous reader knows, none other than the old women. Lord Cawdor, at the head of his forty yeoman, trotted close under Carnunda, the stronghold of the enemy, who could, if they had possessed guns, have swept them all off the face of the earth. As it was they narrowly escaped falling into an ambush. A force of French soldiers were lying in wait for them a little further up the road, and had Lord Cawdor taken this route, as was his lordship's first design, his men might have been surprised, though even in that case we may well believe they would have given as good as they got.

However, darkness falling suddenly, caused a change of plans; Lord Cawdor and the reconnoitring party rejoined the main body, and the British troops took up their quarters for the night in Fishguard.

THE ROYAL OAK AT FISHGUARD.

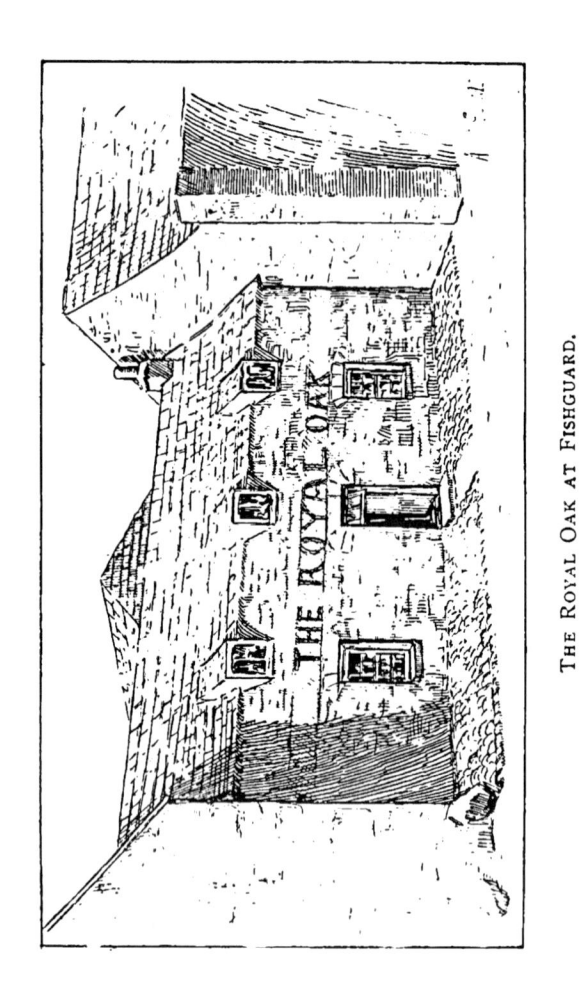

CHAPTER VII.

GENERAL TATE'S LETTER.

I ALSO retired to Fishguard in order to calm my mother's mind about my safety—and also to get my supper.

My mother was, as mothers are, overjoyed to see me, and gave me an ample and excellent supper, liberally seasoned with more hero-worship. I really believe she thought me capable of facing and fighting the whole French force single-handed, and she considered that I had guided Ann George through untold dangers into safety. The other way would have been much nearer the truth, but she did not see it so.

Ah well! after-life has nothing half so sweet in it as that first truest love; and a little knocking about against the harsh angles of the world soon takes off the undue self-esteem it may have fostered. All I know is, I would be glad to have somebody who believed in me utterly now.

The times were too exciting for a lad of my age to sit with his toes under the table; my mother, too, was busily engaged in making preparations to receive the strangers who were quartered in our house, so as soon as supper was ended I fared forth into the street again to pick up scraps of intelligence, and try to find out the latest news.

I was too full of excitement to care to go to bed, and I found most of my fellow-townsmen were of my mind in this matter. I turned in first at Jemima Nicholas's house to see how she and her niece were getting on after their novel experience of warlike tactics on a large scale. Jemima, an immensely powerful woman, seemed only sorry that they had not come to close quarters with the enemy: she was truly a Celtic Amazon who took a pleasure in fighting for fighting's sake.

Nancy, to my surprise, seemed to have been indulging in the luxury of tears.

"What on earth is the matter with you, Nan?" I asked, with unfeeling openness. "Your eyes are quite red."

Nancy shot a glance of anger at me from the orbs in question, but vouchsafed no answer.

"Why, don't you know," interposed Jemima, "that her young man was wounded in the fight up there just now?"

"D'you mean Davy Jones?" I asked. "Oh, I knew one of the sailors got shot; but I didn't know which it was; I never thought of inquiring."

"You unfeeling young heathen!" burst out Nancy. " But there, it's no good talking; boys have no more heart than cabbages."

"A cabbage *has* a heart, Nancy," I retorted.

"Well, so've you—much the same sort," cried Ann, too cross for similes or logic.

Very much offended, I got up, but delivered this shaft before I departed: "*All* those sailors were my friends equally, so it made no odds to me which of them was wounded. And how was I to know Davy Jones was your young man, when it's my belief you didn't know it yourself yesterday."

But the door slammed abruptly just behind my more backward leg, and the rest of my remark was cut off.

I wended my way into the main street, and soon found the centre of attraction to be the old hostelry, the "Royal Oak." Men and boys, and many of the gentler sex also, swarmed round its window and its quaint old porch. The interior was filled with officers discussing the position of affairs. With a good deal of trouble and squeezing, and being in those days of an eel-like figure, I slipped and shoved myself close to one of the windows, where, balancing on my hands and with my nose glued to the pane, I inspected all those men of mark, and tried to find out what their intentions might be.

This position might, affording as it did ample opportunity for the horse-play of the rude, seem *infra dig.* to those who have only known me in my later years; but it must be remembered I was then but a boy not given to stand on my dignity and strongly moved by curiosity, or perhaps I might call it by the higher title—desire of knowledge.

For a good space there was not much

to observe, save the various uniforms of the gentlemen and their manner of taking snuff and of laying their hands on their swords. Of a sudden I felt rather than heard a thrill of excitement in the crowd behind me : this soon resolved itself into a most unmistakable pushing and making-way on the part of some, and of craning forward and tiptoeing on the part of others around me.

With difficulty I turned my head, and I beheld a most unexpected sight. Two French officers were striving to make their way through the hindering, turbulent crowd, the nearer members of which shrank from them as though they bore with them the plague, while the more distant ones pressed forward to catch a sight of these foreigners in the same way that people like to gaze on the more savage members of a menagerie. This caused the strange lurch, the ebb and flow in the crowd. But still the men kept on making for the door of the inn, and no one actually opposed their passage.

One of them carried in his hand a white flag, and almost before I could believe the evidence of my eyes—for the ears had no work to do, every one being too much astonished to speak—the two envoys from the French camp were disappearing through the entrance and being ushered into the presence of Lord Cawdor and his officers.

Now I had reason to be proud of my 'vantage-place. Once more my face was pressed, with considerable outside pressure indeed, against the pane, and I saw with my own eyes that French aide-de-camp, Monsieur Leonard, present, with many a bow and flourish, the written communication from his general to Lord Cawdor. At the sight of those grimaces the crowd around me awoke from their trance of astonished silence—from the absolute stupefaction which had possessed them as it had possessed me. Consciousness and speech returned to them, and took the outward form of maledictions.

I, however, was more interested in watching the demeanour of the gentlemen within than of my fellow-townsmen without the house. His lordship, though his back was not so supple as the Frenchman's, still received the letter with every mark of good breeding; and after a few formalities opened the communication.

"Mark all they do!" I whispered to one of my rib-bending neighbours, who, being of a higher class and better parts than the rest, I imagined would understand me. "Mark it well, Mr. Evans, for this is how History is made!"

"History!" repeated Mr. Evans, blankly. "History happened long ago; this is only to-day."

"Hst!" said the crowd.

In fact, Lord Cawdor had now commenced to read the letter aloud to his officers. It was, happily for us outsiders, and perhaps even for some of the gentlemen within, in English; for the leader of the invaders, being an Irishman, probably understood English at least as well as French, while most of us understood it a good deal better. The letter was short: it was briefly a proposal for the surrender of the entire French force, on conditions. As I had subsequently the privilege of seeing it, I give here the actual words of the letter:—

"CARDIGAN BAY,
    "5*th Ventose*,
        "5*th Year of the Republic.*
"SIR,—The circumstances under which the body of troops under my command were landed at this place render it unnecessary to attempt any military operations, as they

would tend only to bloodshed and pillage. The officers of the whole corps have, therefore, intimated their desire of entering into a negotiation, upon principles of humanity, for a surrender. If you are influenced by similar considerations, you may signify the same to the bearer, and in the meantime hostilities shall cease.

"Health and respect,

"TATE, *Chef de Brigade.*"

Lord Cawdor, however, did not signify the same to the bearer, but a slight smile lit up his features, while the French officers went on to explain that they were ready to capitulate on condition that they should be sent back to Brest at the expense of the English Government. A low murmur broke out among the onlookers. The Frenchmen's ships had deserted them and they wanted us to give them a free passage home.

But Colonel Knox had something to say to that. The uncertain light of lanterns and candles (mostly dips, for the resources of the "Royal Oak" and, indeed, of Fishguard, were limited) fell on his white hair and handsome uniform, flickering on the gold of the embroideries, and no one but those who knew would have believed that his fancy was as brilliant as that glittering braid.

"We have ten thousand men now in Fishguard," said he, "ten thousand more are on the road. Unconditional surrender are our only terms."

The messengers looked very blank when they understood the tenour of these words, but they appeared still more impressed when Lord Cawdor in a stern voice, but with his usual courtesy of manner, gave them an answer. He informed them that he should at once write an answer to General Tate, which he should send to him in the morning, but that they might tell him in the meantime that his troops would be expected to parade for surrender on the following day.

His lordship, who had hitherto been standing, sat down and consulted for a few moments in an undertone with some of his suite. Then taking up a pen, he quickly wrote an answer, dusted sand over it to dry the ink, and standing up once more he read it aloud in clear and ringing tones. It commanded the admiration and approbation of all present on both sides of the window, except perhaps of the aide-de-camp and his fellow, who probably did not understand the English tongue, and if they had would not perchance have admired the style of the composition. We did, however—that is, those of the crowd who heard it—and the rest taking it on trust, we signified our approval by three cheers, delivered with excellent intention, but in the usual disjointed Welsh fashion.

Lord Cawdor merely remarked in his letter that with his superior force (save the mark!—and the old women!) he would accept of no terms except the unconditional surrender of the whole French force as prisoners of war. And that he expected an answer with all speed, this being his ultimatum: Major Ackland would present himself at the camp at Trehowel early on the following morning to receive this answer, for which Lord Cawdor would not wait later than ten o'clock.

These were the actual words of the letter which was delivered on the following morning at Trehowel to General Tate and six hundred Frenchmen, drawn up in line, by his lordship's aide-de-camp, the Hon. Captain Edwardes, his white flag of truce being carried by Mr. Millingchamp.

"FISHGUARD, *Feb.* 23rd.

"SIR,—The superiority of the force under my command, which is hourly increasing, must prevent my treating upon any other terms short of your surrendering your whole force prisoners of war. I enter fully into your wish of preventing an unnecessary effusion of blood, which your speedy surrender can alone prevent, and which will entitle you to that consideration it is ever the wish of British troops to show an enemy whose numbers are inferior. My major will deliver you this letter, and I shall expect your determination by 10 o'clock, by your officer, whom I have furnished with an escort who will conduct him to me without molestation.

"I am, &c.,

"CAWDOR."

The major referred to was Major Ackland

who accompanied Captain Edwardes to Trehowel.

We thought it very fine—and so it was; and the words we didn't understand we thought the finest. After this the French envoys were dismissed, with their white flag still grasped firmly. They were also provided with a strong escort to take them back safely to their own lines, and indeed they required it, for by this time we had quite wakened up; and as the two men were led forth from the inn blindfolded with thick shawls lest they should spy the poverty of the force, we greeted them with a yell which must have made their hearts shake. My countrymen are beyond all comparison better at yelling than at cheering; it was cowardly no doubt of it, considering the difference of our numbers; but when was a mob anything but cowardly?

Of course to a boy it was pure delight, and

my enjoyment that evening made up for the cramp of the night before. The escort kept us at more than arm's length, but no friendly force could have kept us from running after these representatives of the enemy, or from shouting at them, or even from throwing a few stones and sticks at them. The men remembered the wine and brandy, the women the slaughtered ducks and geese, and they hurled stones and curses mixed at the two devourers we could get at. The escort certainly received the brunt of the battle and most of the stones, and sent back many objurations at us in return; but we were too hurried to discriminate friend from foe.

We ran as far as a place called Windy Hall,[1] from whence there is a wide-stretching view of Goodwick Sands and the most per-

[1] Now in the possession of Mr. Brett, the well-known artist.—EDITOR'S NOTE.

fectly-exposed down-hill slope that could possibly be desired for the final volley of stones with which we wished them goodnight.

I was pretty well tired out by this time, so returned home to see how my parents fared in these strange days, and to have a second supper, and then to bed in my own particular little den, which usually I had only the felicity of occupying in the holidays: and so the Thursday came to an end.

FRIDAY.

THE THIRD DAY.

CHAPTER VIII.

THE GATHERING AT GOODWICK.

Not many hours did the little den hold me after all, for in the early morning I woke with the feeling that something strange was astir. Then came a vague terror — the memory of my yester-morn's awakening, and then a sense of jubilant triumph as I recalled the Frenchmen's offer and the stout answer of our chief. Surely they would capitulate now without more talking or more fighting. I should have liked to have witnessed a little fighting well enough—from a distance. But then a fight is a very uncertain thing, it twirls about so, you never know where it will get to next, or where you are sure to be in it, or still more, safe to be out of it.

The men quartered in our house were astir early, and perhaps their heavy footfalls had more to do with rousing me than my own excitability. Still quick-silver seemed to be running about all over me as I hastily swallowed my breakfast—which, however, I did full justice to—and then rushed out of the house to join everybody else on the road to Goodwick. What a throng there was! Every man, woman, and child in Fishguard and all the country round seemed to have turned out, and to be making for the great sands at Goodwick. The people gathered from every direction, east, west, and south, until the semi-circle of hills was dark with them. Chiefly, however, the throng came from the east and south, for Trehowel lay to the west, and there were but few of the natives left in that direction ; besides which the steep white road that mounts the hill on that side of the sands was left clear for the descent of the enemy. No one wished to interfere with them needlessly; quite the contrary: at all events, till they had got within reach of our trained men. In the meantime we would give them a wide berth lest they should turn and rend us.

Suddenly a wild voice and a wild figure smote our senses—both eyes and ears.

"The dream, the dream!" it yelled. "The dream is coming true!"

"What dream? What is it?" asked every one, but there were more askers than answerers.

"Use your ears and listen!" continued the wild voice. "Use your eyes and see!"

"Whoever is he, Jemima?" I asked, finding myself near a reliable woman. Nancy stood some little way off leaning against a cart.

"Why, it's old Enoch Lale," said Jemima. "I know him well enough, he lives over there under Trehowel, by Carreg Gwastad, just where these blacks landed."

Why Jemima always persisted in calling the French "blacks," I know not; possibly because they were foreigners, possibly she meant blackguards.

"My dream! I told it to ye, unbelieving race, aye, thirty years ago!" yelled the old man.

"'Deed, that's true for him," remarked Jemima.

"I heard him tell it many a time, years and years ago. Well, I always thought he was soft, but now he seems real raving."

"Thirty years ago I had the vision, and you know it, men and neighbours."

"Yes, yes, true for you, Enoch Lale," answered many a voice in the crowd; chiefly this response came from elderly persons who had doubtless heard the tale many a time.

"But I haven't heard it. I wasn't born then," I remarked.

Whether Enoch Lale heard this gentle protest, or whether he was resolved not to be baulked of his story, I cannot say. "I only know," he continued, "I had a vision of the night, and the future was revealed to me in a dream; yea, and more than a dream, for I rose up out of my bed and went down on to the rocks and there—on Carreg Gwastad— the French troops landed, and I saw them— aye, as plain as ever any of you saw them two days ago. And that was thirty years ago, yet it has come true! But wait, and listen! and ye shall hear the brass drums sounding, as I heard them sound that night! Listen! Listen!"

"Come down off that cart and be quiet, Enoch Lale, or you'll be having a fit. We all know, you've told your dream often enough; why you woke me up that very night to tell it."

And the prophet was taken possession of by a quiet elderly woman, his better half.

"Well, we got rid of old I-told-you-so rather suddenly," I observed to Jemima. "But it is very queer about his dream."

"There's a many things," replied Jemima, "as we don't know nothing about — and dreams is one of them."

It was marvellous to watch the gathering of troops and people. The hill to the south of the bay were covered with peasant men, and the red-whittled women who had done such good service to their country, and whose conduct has never been rewarded by any faintest token of gratitude or even of recognition by that country.

At the foot of these hills came a marsh, bounded by a road on the other side of which were the famous sands—where were stationed in a compact body the Castle Martin Yeomanry Cavalry. Ere long these men were drawn out of their trim ranks for a difficult and dangerous duty ; but of that anon.

The infantry was drawn up in a field on the east side of the bay, just under Windy Hill, to which farm the field belonged. The force consisted of the Cardiganshire and Pembrokeshire Volunteers — about three hundred strong: together with the Fishguard Fencibles. Numerically weak we were indeed, but on our own ground and with right on our side. Added to which we had had the pleasing news of the enemy's faintheartedness : so that altogether we felt ourselves animated by the courage of lions.

Major Ackland had had his promised interview with General Tate in the early morning at the French headquarters in the old house of Trehowel. The interview had been a short one, and much to the point; he declined altogether to parley, or parlez-vous. He insisted on instant and unconditional surrender; then sticking spurs in his horse he galloped away without any compliments.

Lord Cawdor and his staff were riding up and down the sands when the gallant Major appeared bringing the glorious news that the French were coming, and at once, and that they were prepared to surrender at discretion. But the Colonel still continued his work of inspecting the whole of the British troops. He still thought, perhaps hoped, that there might be a passage of arms.

Then came a time of deep silence when each individual among us concentrated his senses in his ears. I, being but a boy, allowed my eyes a little freedom; most other eyes were concentrated on the road where the French would first appear, but I permitted mine to gaze around me, when I at once made a discovery. The cart against which Nancy had leant contained a man, the outline of the back of whose head seemed strangely familiar to me. I could only see the back of his head for he was leaning out of the cart with his face turned away from me, but towards another person who was standing on the other side of the cart. Some bushes, behind which the cart had been drawn up, prevented a clear view, so I shifted my position a little—in fact, went straight up to the group, who seemed to be placing rather a blind confidence in their retired situation, and in the magnetic attraction of the enemy. I rounded the cart; the young man was, as I had imagined, Davy Jones, wounded foot and all; the young woman was, as I had guessed, Nancy George. Their heads were very near together, perhaps they were talking about splints.

"Why, Nancy!" I exclaimed, "is that you?"

"Yes, of course it is, Master Dan—and why shouldn't it be?" cried Nancy, as red as a turkey-cock, and as inclined to show fight.

"Oh, all right. I only thought you must be somebody else," I returned, politely.

Davy broke into a roar of laughter, and Ann, in spite of her indignation, showed her row of white teeth.

"Go away, you tiresome boy, and look out for the French," was her recommendation.

"And not for the——" but my sentence was cut short by a shove from Nan's vigorous arm which sent me flying for some paces.

"Take care of the spoons, Ann!" was my parting shot, as I made my way a little further down the hill.

We all sat down on the ferny slopes and

waited and listened. As a general rule nobody talked, which showed how grave was the occasion. In front of us was the sea dark grey to-day as was the sky; the sands sometimes almost golden, were, on this dull February day, only another shade of grey; and the great boulders of rock which cropped up everywhere were of the same colour. And this greyness seemed to suit this scene better than the brightness of Wednesday would have done; for though it was a day of triumph to us we could not forget that it was a day of humiliation and bitterness to these hundreds of men who were approaching us on the other side of the hill. The tide was coming in, but without any sparkle and dash, sullenly; and the south-west wind blew in gusts the strength of which told plainly of power in reserve: one could feel that it was capable of violence.

So were the people who sat waiting—

apparently quietly—for their enemies, on the hill-slope, which rose into a natural amphitheatre on all sides (save one) of the scene: whereof the flat sands formed the arena or floor. What a place this would have been for one of the old Roman shows; for a moment I seemed to see the gladiators struggling for life or death, to hear the cruel roar of the lions, to watch the fighting, tearing, and rending in the arena, and to witness what struck me most with awe—the fierce lust for blood which filled the spectators, one and all, as they shouted and craved for more—more blood. I woke up suddenly with a start to find I had been dozing on the hillside, where the people were sitting quietly enough, Britons not Romans, perhaps some of them descendants of these very gladiators who had been

"Butchered to make a Roman holiday."

CHAPTER IX.

THE CAPITULATION.

SUDDENLY the listening people caught a far-off sound; it came nearer and nearer rapidly, one's ears seem to go out to meet it.

"Here they come!" came in a hoarse growl from hundreds of guttural throats— speaking of course in Welsh.

"Hst," came the return growl from the other portion of the crowd.

The sound became louder and louder; it was plainly the beating of brass drums. A sort of thrill—sometimes called goose-skin passed over me, and I doubt not over most of my neighbours. Enoch Lale's dream was the thought that stirred us ; there was something of second-sight about it that awed one even in the morning air and among that crowd of living beings. For a minute I saw again the spectral army of Enoch's vision. Then, being a boy, the practical aspect of the matter struck me.

"I hope the wife hasn't taken the poor old fellow out of ear-shot," I observed to Mr. Mortimer, near whom I had placed myself. "He heard those drums thirty years ago, sir —and he'd like to know he was right."

"No doubt, most of us do," assented Mr. Mortimer. "Oh, Enoch's somewhere about, never fear. Hush, my boy, look there!"

All our senses were focussed in our eyes, something shining and moving we saw, and what could that be save the bayonets of the enemy? Still the shrill clanging of the brass drums went on, broken only by the thud of the sea breaking upon the sand. Every head was turned towards the west (even Nancy's and Davy's for I looked to see) towards the rocky stronghold of Carnunda, past the houses and trees of Goodwick, all along the white road which runs like a riband placed aslant on the hill-side.

The glittering points turned the corner and came into full view; it was at exactly two o'clock that the first of the Frenchmen appeared in sight. On they came, a moving mass of dark blue, carrying no colours, neither gay tricolor nor white flag of peace, but beating their drums so as to put a good face on the matter. A moment later this was changed.

As the column rounded the corner of the road, our hills suddenly started into life and their silence was broken by a prolonged yell so fierce and threatening that the French recoiled and then halted. I could not, even at the moment, blame them; there seemed every probability that they would be massacred. The Welsh had jumped to their feet as with one bound, and they were making up for their long silence now, the men all brandishing every conceivable kind of weapon, the women shaking their fists at the invaders and screeching at them at the top of their voices. I had only a pocket-knife about me and concluded to keep that for my bread and cheese, of which I was badly in want at this moment.

Jemima Nicholas dashed past me, rushing down the hill at full speed with a pitchfork in her hands, followed by some other war-like women of her stamp—some of them armed with straightened scythes. I got out of their way quickly. "Come on, my daughters!" yelled the fierce cobbler—for that was her trade—"come on and cut them down into the sea!"

There is no doubt that she certainly

wished to do it, indeed, there was a manifest disposition on the part of the peasantry, male and female, to come at once to close quarters with the enemy. Then rushed a sudden thunder of hoofs along the shore, as Lord Cawdor and his yeomanry galloped in front of the angry people, ordering them back and impressing their commands with the flat of their drawn swords.

Strong guards were also posted in every path that led from the hills to the sands, while the road on which the French were now meditating a hasty retreat was especially strongly guarded by detachments of the Cardiganshire Militia and the Fishguard Fencibles. At last, seeing these precautions against popular fury and that no sudden violence was now likely to occur, the French once more took heart and resumed their downward march and drums. They were accompanied by Lord Cawdor's aide-de-camp, the Hon. Captain Edwardes, and by Mr. Millingchamp, who bore a large white flag of truce; these had already given the order to "open pans and shed priming" and to march on peaceably: and they were obeyed.

Colonel Colby marched his men down from Windy Hill, and as he passed the spot where I was, I heard him say, "Let us all be ready, my boys, perhaps they may disappoint us still."

But the gallant colonel's hopes of a fight were doomed to be unfulfilled—and so were Jemima's—the French troops were thoroughly demoralised and had no fight in them. They marched on to the sands in columns, halted before Lord Cawdor and his staff backed by a handful of men (for most of our troops were employed in keeping back the excited populace), and then quietly laid down their arms and marched on.

When they had thus deposited their old

flint guns some of them looked around them. It is impossible to describe the chagrin depicted on their features when they realised how trifling (numerically speaking) was the force to which they had succumbed. Still greater was the annoyance they experienced when they discovered that the scarlet flash which had so scared them was produced—not by the red coats of a body of regulars—but by the whittles worn by a parcel of women! These individuals now allowed the fallen foe to have a near view of their tall hats and scarlet mantles, for dashing down the hills on to the sands in spite of the guards (who were indeed too much occupied in looking after the piles of muskets to heed minor matters) these bellicose dames and damsels gathered closely around the Frenchmen, addressing manifold observations to them in their Welsh tongue, in the use of which most of them possess extraordinary fluency.

But their Gallican sisters also can talk and scold. I had by this time got very near to the unlucky commander of the expedition, General Tate; and I was close by when Madame Tate who had accompanied the troops flew at him like a fury. She, too, had discovered the paucity of our numbers, and that Lord Cawdor's "ten thousand men" were—in Spain perhaps—and that the English regulars were—well, very irregular forces attired in scarlet whittles. Her remarks as to the conduct of the campaign were evidently of a most uncomplimentary nature; though I cannot say I understood French, I understood that. In my heart I felt sorry for General Tate.

"Look here, mum," I ventured to remark, "if you want to have it out with somebody, here's a lady of your own weight and age. Tackle Jemima."

Madame Tate, though understanding

never a word, turned furiously on Jemima, who returned the shower of epithets. The General, giving me a look of pure gratitude, hastened away, and I followed his example.

The troops were marched away in columns by fours, and, guarded by our men, set off at once for their various destinations—chiefly gaols; our bands now taking up the strain and making the welkin ring with joyous airs, to which we added all our lungs' strength of voice in songs and cheers.

So ended the famous capitulation of the French on Goodwick Sands.

CHAPTER X.

TREHOWEL ONCE MORE.

WE could still hear the festive strains of "The Girl I Left Behind Me,"—every road was full of soldiers—guards and guarded, some on their way to Haverfordwest, some to Milford, some to Carmarthen, some, for the present, only as far as Fishguard. Their number (sixteen hundred, without stragglers who dropped in later) taxed the resources of this thinly inhabited country to the uttermost, both as regarded the food and the housing of their prisoners. Vast relief was felt when the greater number of them were shipped off to the place from whence they came.

"Where are you going, master?" asked Ann George, coming up to Mr. Mortimer as he was moving away, having now beheld the end of this strange scene of the bloodless surrender of sixteen hundred men to a very insignificant force; surely one of the strangest sights ever witnessed on the shores of this happy island.

Nancy had taken no part in the action of her aunt Jemima; she was not the woman to jeer a fallen foe, so she had remained quietly by the cart till all was over, then had turned to her master.

"Where are you going, master?" asked the faithful servant.

"Back to my own house; for I suppose it is mine again now," said he, with a sort of groan as he thought of the manner in which the old home had been desecrated.

"I'll come too," said Nancy, "the place is bound to be topsy-turvy, sir, and a gentleman can't do aught to straighten it. I'll come too."

"Better not, Nancy, there are a lot of drunken vagabonds about still—too drunk to know they've capitulated. And some of the officers who were afraid to trust to the white flag and our word are at Trehowel still."

However, Nancy was not to be put off so; she would go. She had been in service for some years at Trehowel and she considered that the kitchen belonged to her, and it went to her heart to think of the damage done. She could have no peace till she could begin to repair it, and to set things once more in order to receive home the bride, as now the strangely postponed wedding would surely take place.

Davy Jones went too—I suppose because Nancy did; they seemed great friends now, though previously the young woman had been in the habit of giving him the cold shoulder, I imagine because of his habit of smuggling ; but I did not take much interest in the matter as a boy, not understanding the fair sex ; indeed, even in after years I doubt if I ever quite succeeded in fathoming their method of reasoning. However, it is quite certain that as Nancy permitted it Davy was quite content to go wherever she did, and he gave her and me also a seat in his cart. I went too, for I thought that if there was anything to be seen I might as well see it ; and I had heard that General Tate had gone back there after the surrender—on parole. I had some curiosity to see him again, and I thought it due to myself to witness the end of this affair, of which I had chanced to see the very beginning.

As we went up the steep hill from Goodwick, we were joined by a party of the Fishguard Fencibles, sent to look after the scattered inebriates, and to take the swords and words of the retiring French officers. When we got to Brestgarn we encountered the grinning face of Llewellyn, about whom Nancy and I had had many an uneasy thought. He told us that his captors had not ill-treated him beyond making him work for them, that they had kept a sharp eye on him for a day and two nights and then he had managed to escape. He had hidden for a while, but as soon as possible had returned to look after his master's goods. Llewellyn was a very ordinary looking man with un-polished—even uncouth manners, but it struck me that he had a stronger sense of duty than is usual.

A few steps further brought us to Trehowel. Out rushed all the dogs, barking, jumping, tail-wagging—absolutely wild with delight at the recovery of their own master. A grey-haired gentleman came

TREHOWEL, GENERAL TATE'S HEADQUARTERS.

forward and addressed Mr. Mortimer with much courtesy—

"Sir, the dogs know you. I presume you are the master here?"

"I was so once. Down, Gelert! Quiet, Corgé!"

The officer then introduced himself to Mr. Mortimer as General Tate. He went on to say that he had understood that the Welsh people were ripe for revolt and that they might march throughout Wales and even a good deal further with wooden swords. That it had been a great disappointment to him to find this was not the case, that it had also been a source of annoyance to him to be deserted by his ships, but that *the* most unpleasant sensation he had ever experienced had been the failing of heart he had felt as his foot touched Welsh soil.

I listened with all my ears to this interesting discourse, which happily I was able to understand, for General Tate being an Irishman spoke English perfectly.

Our attention was diverted by a cry—a cry of surprise which broke from Nancy with a suddenness which startled all of us. We all turned hastily round and beheld the girl standing as if petrified, with her arm stretched out and her hand pointing towards a man who stood a few yards from her— apparently one of the stragglers among the French soldiers, for he was clothed in the same way as the majority of them—a British soldier's uniform which had been dyed a rusty brown. The man looked dumbfoundered but Nancy found her tongue.

"So it is you, James Bowen, who have betrayed your own people to strangers. Uch a fi, traitor ; I could strike you where you stand!"

"Shall I do it for you, Nancy?" suggested Davy, ready to hobble out of the cart.

"No, he is not worth it. Let him go to gaol with his friends," said Nancy, scornfully.

James Bowen looked utterly bewildered; he had evidently been drinking heavily and had not even heard of the surrender; had he done so he would hardly have come back to Trehowel, but would have made off into the interior. But Nancy's contempt roused him somewhat.

"It was your own fault," he said, sullenly, "you drove me away from here, you drove me to the bad."

"And I suppose I drove you to steal a horse and then to break out of gaol, and to run off to France, and to fetch back foreigners here—showing them the entrance to Carreg Gwastad Creek! I helped in that too, perhaps?"

"You needn't pretend to be so particular, you've taken up with a smuggler yourself," growled James.

Nancy's face flamed, but she took a step nearer to Davy and placed her hand in his defiantly.

"It is truth indeed, and I'm going to marry him too, for if he is a smuggler, he is an honest boy and isn't a traitor. I'd have thought nothing of the horse or the gaol—but to betray your own people to strangers—let me get out of the sight of you. 'Cursed for ever and throughout all ages be the traitor.'"

And with this vigorous denunciation of a crime so utterly hateful to the Welsh people, that they even abhor giving evidence in a court of justice, Nancy turned her back on the traitor at once and for ever, and hastily entering her domain at Trehowel, proceeded to restore the silver spoons to their own place.

The kindly dusk hid much of the damage that had been done; and after three days' absence, at the same hour as when she had quitted it, Nancy George was restored to the sovereignty of the kitchen at Trehowel.

And so ended in gladness of heart and rejoicing, Friday the 24th day of February, 1797; and so ended in pain and tribulation to themselves the three days' invasion of the French at Fishguard.

SEQUEL.

THE GOLDEN PRISON AT PEMBROKE.

CHAPTER XI.

THE GENERAL THANKSGIVING.

As I have already mentioned, some of the prisoners were sent to Haverfordwest Gaol —which, being situated in the old castle, was a commodious and roomy resort ; others were placed, temporarily, in the churches of St. Mary, St. Thomas, and St. Martin : others again were sent to Carmarthen, under the escort of the Romney Fencible Cavalry, the officers being conveyed on horseback and allowed their parole ; but the greater part of the French force finally found themselves confined in the Golden Prison at Pembroke. They were taken there and also to Milford by water; and not a few died on board the vessels, being closely shut up under deck. Finally, five hundred of them were safely landed and incarcerated in the Golden Prison, the state of which, with all this overcrowding, could hardly have been so delightful as its name might lead the imaginative to suppose.

Here we will leave them for awhile, returning once more to myself and my own belongings. My kind mother would not let me return at once to my master at St. David's, she looked upon me as "her miraculously preserved boy," and must keep me for a bit to gloat her eyes upon. My father, being a man who loved a quiet life, consented. And so I was still in Fishguard when the Royal Proclamation came down, which commanded us to set aside a day of general thanksgiving for our preservation from the dangers which threatened our beloved country. This command reached us about a fortnight after the danger had passed, posts being rather slow in those days. Indeed, had we had to wait so long for more substantial help, we had been in parlous straights long since. However, "All's well that ends well"—and we had fared through, by the aid of Providence, our own exertions, and the brandy-laden wrecks.

So we all repaired to our several parish churches; my mother hanging proudly on my arm, and regarding me as one to be specially thanked for. Indeed, I was not ill-pleased myself to perceive some nods of heads and pointings of fingers among the old crones and young maids as we passed along. This feeling seemed also to actuate Davy Jones, who limped along arm in arm with Nancy; she, even then not assuming the dependent position, but giving him her arm, as it were, in order to help him along.

She even explained to us that, it being her "Sunday out" she had come all the way from Trehowel for this purpose. I may own that I distrusted that limp of Davy's; it struck me he liked to play the maimed hero.

"Why, Davy," I remarked, very audibly. "I saw you at market on Friday, and you weren't limping a bit. Do you want to have the old women to look at you or Nancy———."

"To arm me?" said Davy, with a wink. "That's it, my boy. What's the old women to me? But Nancy———."

Here Nancy stopped the dialogue by dragging her admirer forward in a most hasty manner, with but slight regard for his wounded limb. The service proceeded as usual. The hymns occasionally tailed off into one voice which quivered and sank, dying out into silence; for as it was well known that the parson's daughter received a shilling from her sire for pitching up the tune again every time it died a natural death, no one liked to be so crooked as not to assist nature when the melody became weak and low. Then the clear young voice came forth and we started afresh. I need hardly say there was no instrumental music.

We proceeded, then, in spite of the special occasion in much our usual manner, leaving most of the thanksgiving to parson and clerk, and lolling about at our ease thinking of nothing, when attention! we heard galloping hoofs along the street, which ran outside the church. At the gate, the horse was suddenly reined up on his haunches—a man flung himself off heavily, and quick feet came tearing up the path to the porch. In an instant every man, woman, and child in the church stood upright, ready for fight or flight.

The door burst open, and the express

messenger rushed in, booted, spurred, and breathless.

"The French! the French!" was all that he could gasp. He was surrounded in an instant by eager questioners, his voice was drowned in a very Babel of noise.

Our worthy divine then assumed command of his congregation. He despatched the clerk to the vestry for a drop of brandy, and then standing square and upright in the pulpit he commanded the people to be quiet, and to allow the man to come unhindered into the pulpit, from where he would himself announce the news. These orders were obeyed, and John Jones having returned with the spirit, the parson administered it, and then desired the man to deliver his message.

It was briefly this; sundry large ships of war, filled with French troops, were making their way up St. George's Channel straight for the port of Fishguard.

In an instant the cry rang through the church—" To arms! to arms!"

Then what a scene of confusion arose, fury, dismay, oaths and shrieks all mingled together, some women fainting, some in tears, the men roused and excited to the uttermost.

" Don't go, don't go, my son," sobbed my mother; but curiosity overcame prudence.

" I'm not going to fight, mother, never fear, but I must go and look on," was my answer.

" Oh Dio, not again, not again!" urged Nancy, thinking of the single combats.

" I'm not going to walk across the sea to tackle a frigate, I promise you," said Davy, with a laugh. But Nancy was not to be put off so.

" All right, come. I'm coming too," she said, and in another instant they were without the church door, where, indeed, we all found ourselves shortly. We tore down to the cliffs as the possessed swine might have raced ; many of us ran to man the fort, but I remained on the higher ground where I could have a better view and see further out to sea.

And soon there was indeed a fair sight to see. Coming round the headland to the west of us, their sails filled with the brisk March breeze, appeared a stately squadron moving proudly under British colours ; but having seen something like this before, some of us still doubted. The fort saluted, and this compliment was returned by the men-of-war without any changing of colours. We began to feel reassured, and soon our hopes were verified. A boat put off from the nearest ship and was rowed to shore in a style that swore to " British tar." The officer landed and explained that the squadron was part of the Channel Fleet, sent to our assistance, and that it was under the command of the brave Sir Edward Pellew. We were very proud of the help rendered us by England, even though it had come a little late, but that was the fault of our roads not their goodwill; and though it had occasioned a worse scare than the real thing, but that was only our disordered nerves which acted up to the old proverb—"A burnt child dreads fire."

The officer inquired very particularly as to the probable whereabouts of the French ships—the three frigates and the lugger. About this we could give him no information whatever. All we could say was, that the French left their anchorage at Carreg Gwastad on Thursday, the 23rd of February, at noon, and took a course directly across the channel towards the coast of Ireland. Our little sloops did not care to venture too near since one of them, the *Britannia*, had been taken by the enemy, the cargo appropriated, and the sloop scuttled and sunk. They were, on the whole, persons to whom it was pleasanter to give a wide berth.

We heard afterwards that one of the ships struck on the Arklow Banks, she was much injured and lost her rudder; one of her companions took her in tow and made for France. They got as far as just off Brest, and then, in sight of home, cruel fate overtook them in the shape of two English ships, respectively under the commands of Sir H. B. Neale and of Captain Cooke. These two made short work of the Frenchmen, both ships were taken and brought over to Portsmouth, where they were repaired, commissioned in the British service, and sent to fight our battles, one of them—oh glory for our little town—bearing henceforth the name of " *The Fishguard.*"

The remaining frigate, accompanied by

the lugger, got safely into Brest, where no doubt they were exceedingly relieved to find themselves after their disastrous expedition.

The scare that our squadron had caused extended from St. David's to Fishguard, all along the coast, in fact, from which the big vessels could be seen approaching the land. There were one or two other scares besides this, for our nerves had been shaken, and our imaginations set going; and truly for many a long year after the little phrase "Look out for the French!" was enough to set women and children off at speed, and perhaps even to give an uncomfortable qualm in the hearts of the nobler sex.

CHAPTER XII.

INSIDE THE GOLDEN PRISON.

I WENT at Easter to pay a short visit to two maiden aunts who lived at Pembroke, where they kept a little millinery—shop I had almost said, but that would have vexed their gentle hearts—establishment. They were sisters of my mother, who came from this district, often called " Little England beyond Wales," the people who live there being in fact Flemings, not Cymri, and the language they speak, being a Saxon dialect, is worth studying, not from its beauty, but from its quaintness and originality. Welsh is utterly unknown "down below," as the North Pembrokeshire folks call the southern half of the county. My mother had great difficulty in acquiring even a superficial knowledge of Welsh, and she was always regarded as a stranger in Fishguard, though she lived there nigh upon fifty years. It was probably my early acquaintance with English (of a sort) that made my father decide to bring me up for the ministry.

However, to resume my story—which was strangely mixed up with that of the French prisoners—one of my chief pastimes during my visit to the worthy spinsters consisted in hanging about the entrance to the Golden Prison. The foreigners were allowed to employ their clever fingers in the manufacture of knick-knacks, made of straw, bones, beads, and other trifles, which they sold in order to provide themselves with anything they might require beyond the bare necessaries of life. My good aunts, Rebecca and

Jane Johnson, permitted these articles to be exhibited on a little table in their show-room, where ladies while idling away their time in choosing and trying on finery, might perchance take a fancy to some little object, and bestow some of their spare cash in helping the poor prisoners. What made my aunts first think of doing this kindly act was the representations of their assistant, a pretty young girl named Eleanor Martin, a daughter of the gaoler of the Golden Prison, who had had such a sudden accession to his numbers and his responsibilities.

One day Nellie had occasion to go to the prison with the money produced by these trifles, and she asked me if I would like to accompany her and see the Frenchmen at work. My answer may be readily imagined. So we set forth, and the first person whom we saw when we reached the limbo of incarcerated bodies, if not of despairing souls, was not by any means a repulsive object, being a remarkably pretty young woman, as like Nellie as two peas are like each other.

" Is't thee, Fan ? " asked Nellie. " Where be feyther ? " Then, remembering her manners, she added, " My sister Frances, Master Dan'l."

Frances and I were speedily friends, in fact, the young woman saw too many strangers to be troubled by shyness.

" Feyther's main busy, and mustn't be spoke to," she observed, with rather a knowing look at her sister. " But the turnkey 'll let us in. It's a mort easier to get in nor to get out of this old coop, Mas'r Dan'l."

I quite assented to this proposition, but remarked that I hoped the turnkey would not make any mistake about us.

" No fear," said Frances, " I was born here and knows the ways on it."

"What's that straw for, Frances?" I asked, for I loved to acquire information.

"For the Frenchers to make hats of. I brings them this much most days," she answered, looking down on her big bundle.

I must really have been growing up lately, for (for the first time in my life) an instinct of gallantry seized me, and I offered to carry it for her. She declined in rather a hurried manner.

"I'd liefer car' it myself, thanking you the same. It's no heft at all, and maybe ye'd shed it about."

"Not I," said I, indignantly, my gallantry gone. "Do you think I've never carried a truss of straw before? That's just like a girl. But what's that in the middle of the bundle?" I continued, eyeing it curiously. "Why, it's a bone, I believe!"

Frances threw the corner of her apron over the bundle in a very pettish manner, and to my great surprise grew as red as a poppy. What was there to blush about in a bone? Nell struck in hurriedly—

"Yes, of course it's a bone, Dan. And what could they make their buttons and ivory boxes out of but bone?"

"I'm sure I don't know," I said, not liking to suggest "ivory" for fear, as tempers were ruffled, they might leave me outside.

"Then don't go for to ax silly questions," retorted Nell. "Can us go in, Roche?"

"Ay, my honies," returned Roche, the turnkey, whom we had now reached. "Leastwise you and Fan can, in the coorse of natur; but who be this young crut?"[1]

"Oh, missus' nevvy he be, as wants to see the Frenchers at work. 'Tis only a young boy, but we'd just as lief let him stay if you'd liefer not let him in."

I did not feel grateful to my young friend

[1] *Crut*, probably a contraction of *creature*.

for this suggestion, which, however, was probably dictated by the wiliness of woman.

"Oh, take him in there, and leave him if you've a mind, my beauty. I reckon one more won't make no odds in there."

This he seemed to consider a first-class joke, for he guffawed till we were out of hearing.

After passing through a guard-room, in which there were several soldiers smoking and lounging about, who offered no opposition to our passing, Fan and Nell being of course well known in the prison, we found ourselves in a large and very dreary hall, paved with flag-stones and almost devoid of furniture. The inmates, however, seemed pretty cheery on the whole; there were apparently about a couple of hundred of them, of whom some were working, some singing, some playing cards or dominoes— *all* talking. Yes, even the singing ones talked between the verses. The spring sunshine came through the iron-barred, skied-up windows, and, in spite of other discouraging circumstances, these children of the South were (what we never are) gay as larks.

They clustered around my companions with every mark of respect and admiration. I naturally didn't understand their jabber, but one remark which was, I rather think, meant for English, caught my ear. "Zay are—some angels out of—ciel!"

"They say you're angels out of the ceiling. What on earth do they mean?" I inquired.

"We knows what they mean well enough, don't you trouble, my honey," answered Nell, who was more friendly to me than her sister was.

I don't think Fan had got over her annoyance about the bone; she still carried the bundle of straw with her apron thrown over it.

We now went to the part of the room where the men were busy with their manufactures, and here I had really cause for astonishment. With no tools except some wretched little penknives, these skilful-fingered fellows were turning out most lovely work in bone, wood, and slate. Some of them executed beautiful mosaic work by letting-in pieces of various coloured stones on a bed of slate; they afterwards ground and polished the whole till it resembled the far-famed Florentine mosaic. I perceived a grindstone in the corner of the room, which the leniency of the authorities permitted them to have and to use.

Others of the prisoners were deftly plaiting the straw in many fanciful devices, these plaits again being rapidly transformed into hats for men, women, and even dolls. A great many toys were to be seen in various stages of their formation, wooden whistles, ships, dolls, windmills, and many other objects of delight to childhood.

I scanned eagerly the faces of all I saw to discover the countenances of any of my more particular assailants; but I did not succeed in recognising one of them. There was such a remarkable similarity among them, each man was as like his neighbour as could be; all haggard, all unwashed, all unshaven. They excited pity, even in a boy's unsentimental heart; and withal, now that they were not drunk with greed and brandy, they were so lively and merry. I was quite sorry I could not understand their jokes.

Fan did not make over her straw to any of these men, as I fully expected that she would; nor did they seem to expect it. I heard a great deal of talk about Monsieur le Commissaire, and there was a good deal of pointing of fingers and something about "chambre voisine."

As Fanny sheered off I followed.

"Can't I come into the voisin chamber?" I asked, not knowing the meaning of the word, "and see Mounseer the Commissary?"

Fan looked at me in a startled way, but Nell interposed hastily—

"Let him come, he's main quick and might help; he's not a cursëd boy."

I must explain that in this dialect cursed means malicious or ill-natured; it has the meaning, in fact, which Shakespeare followed when he spoke of "Kate the curst" in his "Taming of the Shrew."

Frances looked doubtful, but went on, Nellie and I following. As we entered the little adjoining room a young man jumped up, and, running to Nellie, took her hand and kissed it with much fervour.

"Hallo!" I cried, "what d'you let that common fellow kiss your hand for?"

"He isn't a common fellow—he's an engineer!" cried Nell, angrily, "and you're nothing but a dull young boy not to know a gentleman when you sees one!"

"Beg pardon, mounseer," said I, for Frenchy was bowing to me, and I wished to show we Welsh knew manners. But though he might be a gentleman, I still hold to it, he was grimy.

"I've brought you the money for the things sold in missus' shop," continued Nell; then turning to me, "This gentleman, as is an engineer, is main clever, and manages all the accounts."

The engineer seemed to me to have been clever enough to have managed more than accounts; however for once discretion prevailed and I held my tongue. Then Nellie and this mounseer fell to their accounts, and seemed to have a great deal to say to each other in a mixture of French and English, which, not understanding very well, I found stupid, and turned to look for Fanny and her friend, another grimy individual, who proved to be the commissary himself.

They also seemed much taken up with each other, and were conversing in the same lingo. I noticed that Fan had made over her bundle of straw to this man, and she seemed very busy talking over some arrangements. I approached, being willing to know what it was all about.

" Who ze plague is zis garçon ? " asked the commissary.

" Oh, a young boy from down town—veal, savez-vous ? Nong mauvais—a smart young chap obligant. Can portey kelke chose, vous savez."

" Bon ! " said the Frenchman, letting the word fly out like a shot, " we af some drifles to make car out of zis."

I perceived at once that he had acquired his knowledge of English from Frances, as "car" for "carry" is pure Pembrokeshire.

"I shall be very glad to be of use," I remarked. "What sort of things, Frances—gimcracks, I suppose?"

"Vat says he, là?" inquired the commissary.

"Yes, gimcracks of a sort—rather heavy, though, we find them," said Fan, not stopping to translate. "If you'll lend a hand, we'd get along better."

"All right," said I.

"Zey is kep' in ze bockat," remarked Mounseer, luckily indicating some pails in the corner by a gesture of his hand.

"Adoo, Pierre, I think we'd better alley," remarked Fan. This, I must say, was the sort of French I liked.

"To nex' time, my cabbage!" said Pierre.

Then while they were busy over the buckets I turned suddenly and beheld the engineer bestowing on Nellie an unmistakable kiss.

"Hallo!" I said.

"It's only their foreign ways; like as if we was to shake hands," cried Nellie, running forward and looking very rosy. "Come, catch a hoult on these pails, Dan'l; they're main weighty for we maïds."

I did catch hold of a couple of pails, one in each hand, and found that the last part of Nell's remark was true.

"Just feel the heft of un!" remarked Fanny.

I did feel it a good deal before I had done with it. Nellie also carried a pail, and Frances a large bundle, done up in some old sacking.

"What's all that?" I inquired, as we made our way out of the prison.

"Dirty clothes," said Frances, sharply. "They must have some clean linen, I suppose, though they are Frenchmen!"

It seemed to me that they managed to

exist without it, but as the point was not material, and Frances appeared touchy, I held my tongue.

"This young boy has giv' a hand with the sweepings, Roche," said Frances, as we passed that functionary.

"Ay? Well, you and Nell be pretty well weighted too, surely," drawled Roche.

"Oh, gimcracks, and clothes for the wash-'us (house)," answered the girl lightly, and in another moment we were in freedom—in the open air.

"Oh, poor chaps; how good it is!" said Nellie, drawing a long breath.

We went round to a piece of untidy waste land behind the prison.

"I'll be bound your arms aches," said Frances. "Drop the buckats, Dan'l, and thank ye."

"Here!" said I, "drop your gimcracks on this dirty place—what for?"

"Oh, never mind what for; don't argufy, my boy, them's prison sweepings; the gimcracks is in Nellie's pail."

"Oh, I thought these were mighty heavy gimcracks. Well, let me carry Nell's pail to the shop."

"No, no!" cried Nell, stepping back, "I'd liefer car my own, don't you trouble."

"Then I'll take your dirty linen," said I, making a sudden grab at Frances' bundle.

To my great surprise some bits of stone and a cloud of mortar flew out.

"Hallo!" I said.

"Look here, Dan'l," said Fan, firmly, "we are greatly beholden for your help, but we don't want no more at present. You go on with Dan'l, Nell, and leave me here to empt the buckats."

Nell put down her pail, took my arm, and marched me off. I was inclined to be offended, but she soothed me down as any woman can when she chooses. She assured me that both the engineer (whom she called Jack—probably Jacques was his name) and the commissary had taken a great fancy to me, and would undertake to teach me French if I would only go often enough.

I had not the least objection to going, as I found prison experiences amusing, but I could not quite understand the bucket-carrying part of it.

However, neither flattery nor a curiosity stimulus were unpleasing to me, so I went frequently.

CHAPTER XIII.

AWAY! AWAY!

A COUPLE of weeks passed away thus, when one morning we were awakened early by a clamour in the street. All Pembroke was in an uproar. All that I could distinguish of the cries was one exclamation, "The French!"

Had they broken out, and were they going to sack the place? The panic reminded me of our feelings at Fishguard in the spring, but seemed more strange to me now, for in the *interim* I had become comparatively intimate with the foreigners, and had lost my fear of them. I jumped out of bed, dragged on a garment or two, and flung open my little lattice window.

"Where are the French?" I yelled.

"Away, away!" came the answer. "Clean gone."

The idea occurred to me that if they had gone away clean they must have been in a very different state to their usual condition; however, my reflections were disturbed by the sudden appearance of my Aunt Jane; she burst in head foremost.

"Where's Eleanor?" she gasped.

"Where are the French?" I answered lightly, "Away, away!"

"Are ye cursëd, boy, or only dull?"[1] queried my angry relative. "What d'ye mean?"

"Nothing," I answered; "only I know no more about Nell than I do about the French. Isn't she in the shop?"

[1] *Dull*, stupid.

"In the shop! My patience—she isn't in the house, nor hasn't been for hours. Her bed is cold; I doubt she never got into un, only topsy-turvied un a bit."

"Nellie really gone!" I was beginning to grasp the situation. "Oh, Aunt Jane; she must have gone with Jack."

"Who's Jack, name o' fortune? I heard tell of a Billy and a Tommy, but norra Jack."

"Oh, this wasn't a Pembroke Jack, but Mounseer Jacques Roux, Esq., an engineer."

"A Mounseer!" Words failed my venerable relative; she sat down and went off into hysterics, which brought Aunt Rebecca to the rescue, and in the confusion I sidled down the stairs and escaped.

I made my way through the crowd to the Golden Prison, and here a light dawned, and many things became clear to me. A crowd of people were standing at what appeared to me to be a hole in the ground, about sixty yards from the wall of the prison. I edged myself through the lookers-on till I had reached the hole; it was one end of a subterranean passage, the other end of which doubtless emerged—but a sick qualm came over me, and to make matters worse at this moment I espied—and was seen by—Roche the turnkey. He was looking very small, but assumed an air of bluster when he perceived me.

"Arrest that young chap there," he ordered his assistants. " He was a helping o' they sneaking scoundrels; I see un."

In another moment the two men had me in tow, and being also propelled by the crowd in a few minutes, I found myself inside the Golden Prison. I did not find the place at all entertaining this time. However, there were some magistrates there, and one of them, a Dr. Mansell, ordered the men to loose their hold while he questioned me.

I told all I knew, and at the end was relieved, but mortified to hear him say, "There is no occasion to detain him, the boy evidently knew nothing about it. He was a young ass, but he is not the first of us who has been befooled by a woman."

At this there was a general guffaw in which I tried to join, but I felt as small as Roche the turnkey. It appeared that all those pails and bundles had been full of earth, stones, and mortar, which the men had scraped out in making the tunnel. I went into the little inner room, and there in the floor, just behind where Pierre Lebrun used to sit, surrounded with bundles of straw, blocks of wood, &c., was the other end of the subterranean passage. They had absolutely scratched through the thick wall of the prison, and then grubbed like moles through sixty yards of earth, with no other implement than the bones of horses' legs.

I did not care for the remarks of the bystanders, and I got out of that gaol as quickly as I could, but not before Dr. Mansell had asked me another question or two.

" I hear Frances Martin has absconded," he said. "Can you tell me anything about Eleanor? She lives with your aunts, I think."

"She is not to be found, sir," I answered. "She is off with Jack, no doubt."

" Jack?"

" Mounseer Jacques Roux, the engineer."

" Ah, the fellow who managed the tunneling. Why do you pitch upon him?"

"I didn't—she did, because he used to kiss her."

" Kiss! By George, didn't that rouse your suspicions?" cried the doctor.

"No, sir, they said it was the French way of shaking hands."

" Go along, softy!" cried the crowd, and I

went. But as I went I heard the stentorian voice of Dr. Mansell proclaim—

"Five hundred guineas reward for the recovery of those two young women, dead or alive!"

In a few hours handbills to this effect were posted all over the place, and, as soon as practicable, in every town in the kingdom; by which the names of Frances Martin and Eleanor Martin must have become well known. Whenever I saw one of these placards it seemed to me as if I had had something to do with a great crime, and that part of the five hundred guineas would perhaps be given for my body some day—dead or alive.

I walked down to the shore to a little port on the outside of the town, the very place to which I had been on the previous Sunday with Nell. I remembered, with another qualm, the interest which she had taken in the shipping, and how she had even begged me to ask some questions of the sailors, who, as usual, lounged about where they could smell tar. She said it was awkward for a girl to talk to these rough fellows, but that it was a pleasant variety for a young man. So, of course, I asked all the questions she desired about incoming sloops. I, thinking these questions referred to some sailor sweetheart, took no account of the matter at all. As we looked and talked we perceived a sloop in the offing coming in. The men said she would be in shortly, and that she was bringing culm for the use of Lord Cawdor's household.

Nellie seemed very pleased and happy as she watched the sloop coming rapidly nearer, a brisk breeze from the south filling her sails and urging her onwards. The only boat actually in the harbour was Lord Cawdor's yacht.

His lordship's yacht was now nowhere to be seen; the sloop was still there, for owing to the breeze and the sailors' hurry to get ashore on Sunday, they had run her aground, and there she was hard and fast, but not in the same state as on Sunday. A hundred Frenchmen had made their escape, creeping through their tunnel and jumping out at the other end like so many jack-in-the-boxes. Some of the fugitives made at once for the yacht, some for the sloop, which, to their great disappointment, they found aground. They boarded it, lashed the sailors' hands and feet (these men now recounted the story, each man to a listening crowd, which we must hope was a slight solace for their sufferings)—they took compass, water casks, and every scrap of food and clothing they could find; then conveyed them aboard the yacht which they launched, and off they were. The tied-up sailors had seen nothing of any women, but between darkness and surprise it was a wonder they had noted as much as they had.

This was all that we could gather at the time; it was only enough to make us very uncomfortable about the fate of the two rash girls. My position was not made more comfortable by the constant reproaches of my two old aunts, who seemed to think me in some way responsible for Nell's escapade. Altogether I was not sorry that it was decided to send me back at once to St. David's; school was better than scorn. But the very night before I left Pembroke, my uncomfortable feelings were doomed to be deepened. The stern of the yacht was washed ashore with other timbers, on one of which his lordship's name was inscribed. There could be little doubt of the fate of those on board. The weather had been rough and foggy, and these French soldiers were probably little skilled in navigation. So I departed to St. David's with a heavy heart.

Some weeks passed in the usual course of classics and mathematics rammed in by main force, when one day there came a letter to me in Aunt Jane's handwriting. I was surprised, for my aunts were not given to composition ; but on opening the envelope I found Aunt Jane had written—nothing. She had merely enclosed, oh, greater surprise, a foreign letter. I had never had, and never expected to have, a foreign correspondent. What language would he write in—a quick hope flashed through me that it might not be Latin, any other I would give up quietly.

I opened the letter and perceived it was in English. It ran as follows :—

"DEAR MASTR DANL,—I hope as this finds you well as it leaves me at present.

You was main good to we, so I pens this line to say as I am no longer Eleanor Martin but Madam Roux. [Oh joy! I didn't care what her name was as long as she wasn't drowned.] Yes, me and Jack have married, only he likes it writ Jacques which is a mort of trouble. Howsomever we gets along lovely so likewise do Frances and her young man Peter which were a commisser and she is now Madam Lebrun. We did a main lot for they lads—which they was grateful. Praps you'd like to hear that after we got safe away in his ludship's yat, after you'd kindly helpd we to burrow out o jail, we come in for three days fog. Short commons there was till we overtook a brig, gave out as we was shiprackt and was took aboord, Fan and me dressed as lads. That night we was too many for the crew of the brig, as nocked under and us made them steer for France, so here we be. The brig had corn aboord, so we wasnt clemmed. We let the yat go. Hoping to see you soon, I remains,

"Your humbel servant to command,

"NELLIE."

Her ending wish was granted some years after, when peace was settled between England and France. Nellie and her husband, the engineer, came back to Wales and settled for a time in Merthyr, where they opened a large inn, he following his profession in the mines, both he and his wife roasting me unmercifully when I went to stay with them (a full-fledged curate), on the assistance I had once rendered to the French prisoners in a mining operation; but I hope all will understand that this assistance was unintentional on my part, and that I greatly condemn the unpatriotic conduct of the sisters.